Building Self-Esteem
in At-Risk Youth

Building Self-Esteem in At-Risk Youth

Peer Group Programs and Individual Success Stories

Ivan C. Frank

Westport, Connecticut
London

Library of Congress Cataloging-in-Publication Data

Frank, Ivan Cecil.
  Building self-esteem in at-risk youth : peer group programs and
individual success stories / Ivan C. Frank.
      p.   cm.
  Includes bibliographical references and index.
  ISBN 0–275–95267–3 (alk. paper)
      1. Peer counseling.   2. Self-esteem in adolescence.   3. Youth—
Counseling of.   I. Title.
  BF637.C6F65   1996
  362.7—dc20   95–34414

British Library Cataloguing in Publication Data is available.

Library of Congress Catalog Card Number: 95–34414
ISBN: 0–275–95267–3

First published in 1996

Praeger Publishers, 88 Post Road West, Westport, CT 06881
An imprint of Greenwood Publishing Group, Inc.

Printed in the United States of America

The paper used in this book complies with the
Permanent Paper Standard issued by the National
Information Standards Organization (Z39.48–1984).

10 9 8 7 6 5 4 3 2 1

Nations, like people, come face to face with moments of truth. They too, travel through periods of history that challenge their social fabric. These periods challenge their survival and redefine their values, making them stronger or rendering them lasting damage. In this decade, America is facing such a crisis with its youth. It is incumbent upon all of us to become involved in reclaiming the initiative in order to strengthen the values and direction of our youth. Only in this way will we be strong enough to continue on the path of true fulfillment for all our people and our country.

Contents

viii   Contents

Acknowledgments

I am indebted to many people who assisted me in the creation and writing of this book. Belinda Biscoe, a truly wonderful person and psychologist who works full time with at-risk teens, was a friend and mentor since 1991. Her consultations with the staff of A Chance for Youth helped that program succeed. She also trained volunteers for that program in Oklahoma and wrote the curriculum for such programs. Without her ideas, many of us would not work with the faith that we can have some success with children who are at risk. Aaron Sharon, a social worker in the Tel Aviv municipality who, since 1977, has been explaining and giving me data to demonstrate how the Youth Aliyah Rehabilitation Programs in Kibbutz do even more than reach the goals which they set in the early 1970s, has been an invaluable person in my research during the last sixteen years. I was motivated to write this book because of the achievements that those Israeli programs exemplify.

My colleagues and friends in the History Department at George Westinghouse High School encouraged me and gave me their support for the creative ideas that I used at George Westinghouse High School in the early 1990s.

I also received that important ingredient of administrative support from the principal of the high school, Mr. Lester Young, who had similar goals of building up the resiliency of the students and teaching them how to survive in a difficult time and space situation. I would not have been in a position to write this book without the stories of student teachers, veteran teachers, and psychologists who related some of their own experiences. Each one of those stories, whether from the eastern or western part of the United States, or from other countries, has many positive and esteem-building qualities.

Finally, from 1992 to 1994, my close friends and family reminded me that I reach at-risk youth; and they encouraged me to write this book. In this regard, Barbara Fisher typed and retyped the manuscript until it was finally ready for printing. Her patience and good heart also helped me complete the work on this book. Sam Fleischer, an advisor and renowned psychologist, was also one of those people who provided me with encouragement. So were our daughter Michal and our son Ayal. On a regular basis, my wife Malke listened to my stories, met my students, and never let me quit, even when those difficult times were almost too frustrating to overcome. Most of all, I thank my students who gave me their trust, their insights, and their creativity. It was they who provided me with enough confidence to help them when and as much as I was able.

Introduction

> Crime is the expression of a human soul which is still fighting
> against other's domination while failure, as in school, represents
> a soul already defeated.
>
> A. S. Neill

In the famous draft riots in New York City during the American Civil
War, the *New York Times* admitted that the actual rioting had little to do
with the draft. "It was actually a craving for plunder, a barbarous spite
against a different race" (Tunley 1962, 99). It was reported that three
fourths of the participants were in their teens. The police were unable to
cope with the gangs, which were so numerous that it took five minutes for
all of them to pass one spot in the stampede.

About two years ago, in April 1992, I attended a special workshop
sponsored by A Chance for Youth, a federally contracted outreach
program to help high-risk youth in Oklahoma City learn survival skills.
At that workshop, Dr. Belinda Biscoe, a nationally known psychologist,
explained to staff members and volunteers how peer group pressures
compel teenagers to commit crimes against the public, to inflict damage
on themselves with drug addiction, and to strike out at adults of other
races or even their own peer groups in order to spill out the anger of their
shame.

As many concerned parents and grandparents ponder how to raise
children in the 1990s, they realize that one half of our teenage children
are at risk at more than the normal level. Even when there are two
functioning parents, there remain potential difficulties because of low
self-esteem, school phobia, and experimentation with drugs and alcohol.

The book, *How to Find Help for a Troubled Kid* (Austin and Reaves
1990, 3), presents dynamite statistics, such as that one and a half million
American teenagers are arrested every year for offenses ranging from
murder to truancy; nearly a million and a half run away from home;

several hundred thousand drop out of school; six thousand kill themselves; fifty thousand are admitted to private psychiatric hospitals; over a million have drinking problems; four million smoke marijuana; and of the thirteen million girls in total, more than one million become pregnant each year (400,000 have abortions and 500,000 give birth). (The total number from which James B. Austin and John Reeves drew these statistics was twenty-five million.)

What surprised me, however, was that the authors could only list a few alternative educational programs to help troubled youth who were poor. They did not mention even one developing peer group program for at-risk youth. The only alternative program described in detail, which was outside an urban environment, was Outward Bound. This was considered somewhat successful, although the rough wilderness trips and strict regime have been very controlling and sometimes more dangerous than the "mean streets."

Recently, I was reading a small diary that our daughter had made for me in school at age thirteen. I realized that the images of troubled adolescents were very real for her and for others who themselves had low self-esteem in school. The low self-esteem caused them to act out and rebel, not to be dominated or subdued. They became high-risk youth shortly before or after eighth grade. We now know that this could just as easily happen in third or fourth grade.

Our daughter related well to her preadolescent peers who had difficulties because of their dysfunctional family situations and peer group pressures. Eventually, these problems caused anxiety for us; and it took much patience, good counseling, and a caring group of teachers in a small private school near our neighborhood to solve them. Most families of at-risk youth cannot afford such key social and educational assistance. Most youth in the last decade have not been rehabilitated. Their self-esteem has remained very low and their at-risk behavior, which leads to severe antisocial outcomes, continues to occur. Thus, society has felt the destructive manifestations of their actions.

Since 1976, I have been observing and working with at-risk youth of all ethnic and racial backgrounds who are experiencing behavioral problems caused by social and emotional difficulties. In the late 1980s and early 1990s, some of these children have been rehabilitated through successful peer group programs, counseling, and teaching in alternative educational settings. However, most of these adolescent youth have not been rehabilitated at all.

The punishment for drug and alcohol addiction and gang-organized crimes has been mainly warehousing or institutionalization and has led to violence, injury, and death for the majority of at-risk youth. Most of them have never escaped the failure syndrome which has guided their lives from the beginning. The failure syndrome is one in which the student almost always fails at everything. If, on occasion, the student does succeed, the ability to hold on to that success is short-lived because it is much easier for at-risk youth to return to failure.

The term *high-risk youth* can be viewed as an all-encompassing concept what had been used in the 1980s by only a few social agencies and governmental organizations in America, such as Act Together (a Washington-based organization). Since there are so many negative statements or reactions by young people to society, it is best to analyze the overall concept by first naming and describing the list of categories into which they fit; and second, by giving specific examples of the young people whose background and present situations place them in those categories. The latter will be done as the story of the American youth studied over the last seventeen years unfolds.

Youngsters who feel inferior, deprived, shamed, and frustrated express those feelings through vandalism and stealing. Youth from dysfunctional families often have low academic skills, vague or totally missing career goals, a poor or complete lack of work history, abuse drugs and/or alcohol, and have been involved with the juvenile justice system.

Our society still emphasizes punishment before rehabilitation for crimes which occur because children lack socialization. Children who have had drug or alcohol problems as early as the age of six or seven become involved in substance abuse-related crimes before the teenage years and continue to have conduct disorders well after adolescence. For example, youth under age eighteen were arrested for 87,222 violent offenses in 1980, and in 1981 there were 479,000 youths being held in 8,333 adult jails and lockups.

More recently, in 1990, the following statistics were recorded: 4,173 teens were killed by guns, the highest firearm death rate ever recorded in the United States; in 1990, there was a rate of 105.3 for every 100,000 black male teenagers killed, a rate eleven times higher than a 9.7 rate in 1985; in Allegheny County in Western Pennsylvania, during 1989/1990, a 56 percent increase in homicide or intentional injury to black males occurred in 1989, a rate of 5.8 per 100,000 people were killed in Allegheny County of which 8.5 per 100,000 were men and 26.4 were black males (Fuoco 1993, A1, A2).

These figures prove that violence was growing while incarceration was creating overcrowded conditions in detention centers, such as Shuman Center in Allegheny County. According to a *Pittsburgh Post-Gazette* report (Fuoco 1993), that detention center recently housed 136 percent of its capacity at its 1990 peak.

Experts in drug and alcohol addiction issues agree that recidivism is the order of the day if these children are warehoused to the same degree that children who are abused by parents at an early age fight back as they become older and, in their adult years, abuse their own children. Some support group programs, such as Lend a Hand, now send volunteers to attempt to prevent child abuse by at-risk single parents. Society has finally recognized the degree to which a generation of youth has become the victim of this problem as well.

When working with at-risk adolescent youth in very poor neighborhoods, some outreach organizations, such as A Chance for Youth, had to set up a drug and alcohol curriculum that included:

1. Teaching youth how to manage peer group pressure
2. Teaching the students how to identify and get in touch with their feelings
3. Teaching youth how to improve and enhance their self-esteem.

Such program goals will be described in complete detail in Chapter 1.

The general long-range goals of such a curriculum are to empower at-risk youth and to enable them to take care of themselves internally with regard to their families. Every high-risk teenager whom I have met and with whom I have worked could have had a chance to survive outside the juvenile detention centers or adult jails (i.e., to be free if such goals as those just mentioned had been attained). The achievement of those goals entails years of hard work by caring professionals and volunteers both outside and inside the school system. Such socialization must occur before most of our mainstream classroom teachers can even make a small academic impact on the youth of many of the adolescent stories of 1993.

As this book is being written, the four police officers in the Rodney King case who had been acquitted in Los Angeles in 1992 were being retried. The rioting of 1992 included rock throwing and fire setting by many teenagers who had plenty of rage to release. *"This proves that they think we blacks are not worth anything"* (my italics) one young girl said on April 29, exactly 130 years since the Civil War Draft Riots occurred in New York.

At the same time that those riots were occurring in the Los Angeles area and spreading throughout the United Sates, I saw a dramatic interview with Jim Brown, a hero to many young boys (including gang members in the Los Angeles ghettos). His basic assumption was that to overcome the low self-esteem and ultimate rag of the gang leaders and their followers, athletes, community leaders, educators, and psychologists need to invest much more time than most of us were.

Education and empowerment for the original gang members were his goals and the goals of others who spoke out with responsible voices that weekend. In one more year, that approach was developed in the Midwest and East, just as it had arisen in most communities in California, Texas, New Mexico, and Oklahoma. As long as there are more young black and Hispanic males in all of the United States who become incarcerated and/or warehoused in detention centers than those who attend colleges or post-secondary vocational schools, the potential solutions to their problems and the ability to save and integrate them and tens of thousands of other at-risk youth will not occur.

Later, when I describe some of the individual work of excellent counselors, teachers, and therapists in one-on-one situations, the many true stories of at-risk youth will be recounted. Then the flavor of the real difficulties can be savored by more Americans who truly care. It will be those concerned and committed citizens who will become personally involved in every community's effort to alleviate the pain and to guide teenagers toward rehabilitation and successful citizenry in the next century. Los Angeles has learned this the hard way. Other communities are now beginning to understand the need to concentrate their efforts on those adolescent problems that are so destructive to our society.

Building Self-Esteem
in At-Risk Youth

Chapter 1

Peer Group Programs: Their Goals, Stages, and Techniques

In many cities, peer group techniques to facilitate positive peer group organization of long-range federally funded programs are succeeding to rehabilitate high-risk youth. There are a number of such agencies, such as Eagle Ridge, Three Rivers Youth in Pittsburgh, and Youth Aliyah Rehabilitation Programs in Israel, which have contracted psychologists and counselors to develop curricula and to train others in the use of peer group techniques. There have recently been some attempts by public schools to do the same. All of these special governmental and agency programs have trained regular staff and volunteers in the use of peer group methods to reach specific peer group goals (*Scholastic Scope* 1993). In the better alternative schools such as Boys Town Ranch in Oklahoma or Cal Farley's Boys Ranch in Texas, as well as in some public schools, teachers, counselors, mentors, ex-gang members, and psychologists have begun to reach out to at-risk youth in large numbers. The American propensity to use mentors and tutors who become buddies to at-risk youth has begun to help youth in rural areas, as well as in the traditional urban programs. More than in the past, this has become an adjunct to peer group programs, and it has been very helpful. Group organization by many hard-working counselors, teachers, and preachers has been given an emotional lift since President and Mrs. Clinton have encouraged better summer job programs and serious training programs for at-risk youth. Better training techniques without the Job Training Partnership Act (J.T.P.A.), which is a bureaucratic waste, could provide more decent opportunities for some in-school at-risk adolescents.

Although the Office of Education in Washington has recorded less dropouts overall, an Assistant Secretary in that office readily admitted to me in a letter that there was an increase in minority urban dropouts in the last few years. Peer group counseling over a long period of time can help provide high-risk youth with an advantage in the battle to become free and successful students and workers in an open society that has learned to praise their rehabilitation.

Certainly, there will continue to be environmental factors that play a major role. If more of the difficult work can be accomplished in a supportive setting, then the at-risk youth will eventually become more integrated. However, some techniques described in this chapter have already proven to be effective, even inside urban American communities. In Israel, they have been even more successful, since the educational ideology is supportive of peer group programs, no matter where geographically they have existed. Because the issue of a supportive environment has been largely overlooked or ignored in the United States and because this factor has proven to be a major variable in the success of long-range peer group programs, the United States must immediately redirect its focus.

In the fall of 1992, after a sixteen-year hiatus, I was rehired as a public school teacher in my home town of Pittsburgh. In eight months, I built positive relationships with a number of students. Eventually, a few of the students told me much about the pain in their lives, as well as their goals. In February 1993, I started to learn about specific school and life problems of many at-risk youth in that community. J. said to me that five or ten minutes of high takes the African-American student temporarily out of despair. She also said that she wanted to live in a place where children can play safely. As we spoke that day, other students listened to her. She was serious and well spoken. She also explained to the class and to me in particular that racism made it difficult for her peer group, and that there was not any person who was not prejudiced, not even me, her liberal teacher.

That same day, we read current events about racism in baseball, among judges, and in other countries. Boys who usually never read and/or never showed interest perked up, spoke up, read; and, in general, became involved in discussion. In that short afternoon, I also had to break up a fight and I talked to G. about his goal to enroll at Connelly Trade School to study auto mechanics after his high school graduation.

To develop some good motivation and peer group competition, I developed a recognition system whereby each month I gave an award (usually a modest gift) to the best student for positive attendance, behavior, and academic accomplishments. We also took pictures of the winner. In early March, I was ready to give an award to a boy who had a serious illness the previous year and who often looked in poor health this year. On the last day of March, I told him that he had done well and that he would get the reward soon. At the same time, he told me that he felt ill but did not want to go to the main office to pick up his medicine that had been delivered by a public health nurse. He was signaling to me that he did not want to be a "nerd" and appear weak. Just as I was returning my key to the office later that afternoon, I heard that our principal had been called to the phone because my awardee and a friend had been shot at on the way home from school. Luckily, he ran into a house of a classmate whose mother called the police. No one was hurt this time, but my student had been terrorized. Would he get to school Monday? Would he and his friend, who was allegedly the target, survive the year? Would they be wounded as G. had been the previous fall? For the first time, such violence was touching me personally--all in one day of despair-- expressions of depression and illness of poor children in the ghetto of my livable city. For my awardee, this was as serious a problem as his serious illness had been the previous year.

Later, in early April, I gave two more awards. One was to an alleged wanna-be gang member who, for two days, blurted out how proud she was and even how she loved me. Although she was not considered a high achiever, she had worked hard to receive that praise. This accomplishment and her spontaneous good feelings had enabled her to transcend her day-to-day difficulties and to express pride and love all at one time. However, I had to wonder about her ability to overcome the peer pressure against doing well in school and working her way out of her dangerous neighborhood, eventually to have a productive and creative future. In Chapter 6, I will quote from an article that she wrote as a senior about how others should stay out of gang life.

In all the cases in which I have described a special peer group curriculum, I have identified the authors, the city, and the year the curriculum was developed. In some cases, I had seen good facilitators use the peer group techniques at regional and national conferences of educators. More often, I was trained myself by such excellent facilitators or by the psychologists who trained counselors and teachers to use peer group techniques. This often occurred when I worked for Three Rivers Youth or was a volunteer for A Chance for Youth, as well as when I studied teaching and administration for the Youth Aliyah Rehabilitation Programs in Kibbutz. I realized that few of these excellent trainers had published their own ideas because they were so busy counseling and training others, as well as raising their own children. Therefore, I personally asked them for permission to describe some of their techniques and to tell the stories that explain how they worked to rehabilitate at-risk youth. Other stories of individual counselors, teachers, and mentors will also enlighten the reader in Chapter 3, and they will depict how dedicated and caring people are who work with at-risk children. Chapter 2 outlines the essence of A. S. Neill's anti authoritarian peer group and democratically run school system, Summerhill in England. The Montessori, Lane, Froebel, Freudian, and Jungian traditions of loving children and not punishing them was a strong support system for Neill's ideas. As Neill himself said,"Obedience is tolerable only when it is a mutual contract," when the peer groups of social agency programs or democratically run classrooms or schoolwide governments make the decisions for themselves.

Although good peer group counselors and excellent adolescent teachers and therapists have researched and taught the effects of drugs, alcohol, and cigarettes on at-risk youth, the dangers of these and other addictives are usually dismissed emotionally by people from seven to twenty-five years old. Even if high school students know how addictive cigarettes and alcohol are and how dangerous they are to their health, it is almost impossible to convince them not to smoke or drink. Television, magazine advertisements, billboards, and MTV know how to explain to adolescents that these same addictives create "coolness." In a *New York Times* article (Marriott 1993), a teenage girl, Jennifer O., was described as one adolescent who regularly drank Malt Liquor Forty at "hooky" parties; and she and her friends were able to be high or very comfortable, as one boy explained, by drinking one bottle only. Jennifer drank this beer (brewed with sugar for the extra alcoholic kick) to such a great extent that she was quoted as admitting that she lost her virginity because she got so high from it; but she regretted only that fact. A video that I watched for an hour at a detention center workers' training session showed all the neat tricks that beer commercials use to attract young black women to their particular beverage and to hinder the attempts of these women to abstain from smoking any highly addictive substance.

The Program, A Chance for Youth, countered these commercials and the peer group pressures to drink and use substances by showing antidrug videos in the middle or at the end of basketball practices for boys and girls between the ages of seven and fifteen. The Program also brought in ex-gang members to talk to youth on the subjects of drugs and violence. Such counselor-run programs occurred in churches in the poverty-stricken areas of Oklahoma City. In these communities, A Chance for Youth, which used a special curriculum, also hoped to organize the parents and neighbors to serve as volunteers in many of its activities. In the meantime, the seven- to fifteen-year-olds continued to meet regularly and were organized for interleague games of basketball. At the same time, counselors and volunteers were being trained to work with youth in the target areas and to reach out to involve churches and adults in the community. However, it was evident to the coordinators of these programs that only the best long-range curricula over two or more years would reach the goals of the better rehabilitative and preventative programs for poor at-risk children, whose parents are likely to abuse substances and neglect or abuse their children.

I have also seen some results with gang members for whom a tutoring program was begun by A Chance for Youth in 1992. After some preliminary outings for pizza and sports programs, the counselors and a few volunteers gained the trust of these youth and eased them into a special tutoring program. The Israeli Youth Aliyah Program in Kibbutz has used this preprogram workshop method, which included discussions and work on army bases before it absorbed at-risk youth into two-year rehabilitation programs on *kibbutzim*. In that type of ideological supportive environment in which the real integrative activities with high-risk youth began, the Youth Aliyah Rehabilitation programs have been able to make steady progress through the stages of their programs in order to attain the overall goals of socialization, career development, and ideological commitment to the country.

Other such tutoring, arts and crafts, and outdoor fun programs for young children have been held in churches and community centers. One such successful organization had connected with two groups--first and second graders, and fifth and sixth graders--over a long period of time in South Oklahoma City, at a church which ostensibly had become a community center for all ages. The arts and crafts activities enabled these young people to transcend themselves and to feel integrated as a group of peers in a positive program. I also saw this type of reaction occur in my high school classes in 1993, when arts and crafts were used as techniques to learn about African society and culture. The senior citizen tutors in the South Oklahoma City program developed close relationships with their tutees, in addition to helping them academically. The younger children in this successful program had already learned gang signs from their older brothers and sisters, who themselves had been influenced in 1990 by California gangs. A Chance for Youth decided to develop this church-sponsored activity into a community-based activity as soon as possible.

Such comprehensive programs, which will last for at least a few years, will save many youth from the abyss, especially if counselors, teachers, and mentors can work with them one-on-one or in small groups on a regular basis in the preadolescent years. In one case, the curriculum used by A Chance for Youth included the following goals:

1. To teach students to communicate
2. To teach students how to manage peer group pressure
3. To help students get in touch with their feelings or to identify those feelings and work through them without hurting others or themselves
4. To teach students facts about drug and alcohol abuse, including the legal aspects
5. To teach problem-solving and decision-making skills
6. To teach students about alternatives to drug abuse
7. To teach students about health issues
8. To promote student awareness of treatment facilities and goals.

A minority group family that has a drug or alcohol abuse problem creates feelings of shame in the child. These feelings, in turn, result in rage which manifests as violence against adults and peers. The results of that rage are slaps in the face to teachers and gunfire against enemy gang members.

In working with such groups, one person as part of a team of counselors, mentors, or teachers must work with, not for; come along side, not lead; assist, not control; provide input, not advice; facilitate, not determine; provide additional resources, not additional requirements; encourage, not mandate, respect, not condescend; show concern, not paternalism; empathize, not sympathize. Many successful programs have been administered by A Chance for Youth counselors, but they also learned that some youth would sabotage programs because, even if they enjoyed the sports and counselor peer group activities, they felt that they were undeserving of such positive caring attention because of their family life and their poor attitudes and behavior in and out of school.

I recall one such student who had come to my high school class from another state. At first, he acted bright and interested if I asked a question, but soon he began to join a few acting-out students, who were also bright; and he reminded me that in Florida he had received all Fs and that he personally was the troublemaker in my class. Although he earned a C from me after a month and a half, he could not accept the positive attention; and during the second semester, he hardly ever came to school. When he did attend class, he acted out much more than the others. Having come from a family in which the father raised him but the family moved, this teenager lacked care and stability. I understood that his anger was a result of his dysfunctional family life. He was absent for three weeks, received an F and said that he was soon moving to another city. In thousands of cases, our children will not be able to care for themselves or even survive the mean streets unless good peer group programs can reach them and their communities over a longer period of time than the typical one year that social agencies are usually given by state or county placement authorities. Besides such excellent curricula developed in the 1970s and 1980s, there have been a number of newer programs in the Southwest and East and in countries such as Israel, especially in the early 1970s when Youth Aliyah had begun to rehabilitate at-risk urban youth.

The famous interaction model of the Highfields Peer Group Work Project, as well as many alternative educational programs, succeeded in rehabilitating some high-risk youth, especially when such programs existed for two or more years. In *Children in Chaos* (Frank 1992), I describe in detail how high-risk street youth from South Tel Aviv were integrated into Israeli society. This rehabilitation program in kibbutz was one of Youth Aliyah's many programs, which were originally established to integrate children of the Holocaust. It was based on the *chevrat noar* and the strong *madrich* concepts. The *chevrat noar* has always been the basic peer group concept of the kibbutz movements and usually included up to forty youth. In the Rehabilitation Program of Youth Aliyah, twenty youth aged sixteen began the program in a number of *kibbutzim*. The Program lasted officially two years before army service in the elite *Nachal* units began. The dynamic development through which the Youth Aliyah rehabilitation peer group passes is different from the dynamic development of all other peer groups on the kibbutz and within the framework of *chevrat noar* on *kibbutzim*. The stages that such peer groups pass through will now be outlined step-by-step, since this program has become world renowned in its ability to integrate an extremely large percentage of at-risk youth, not only into mediocre service or physical labor positions, but even into high-ranking army or academic careers.

In the first stage of its development, the *madrich* has to show initiative and flexibility, since in that stage, more than in any other, the group is a separate closed unit. It is at this stage that the *madrich* is the person on whom the group is highly dependent. In the later stages (after six months most groups enter the second stage), the adolescents gain experience and self-confidence; and their initiatives and creative energies are sufficiently motivated to enable them to act with an ever increasing degree of independence. The first stage is referred to as individual adjustment; the second stage, formation of the group; and the third stage, integration.

In the second stage, there are a number of internal crises as conflicts over leadership arise; but by the end of this stormy period, the group is united and has set up permanent institutions of a democratic and egalitarian nature. During the third stage, the peer group is widened to its extreme boundaries and the days of blossoming begin. By this time (usually the last six months of the program), the group gathers force to prepare to handle future tasks. The group is ready to create an independent society (Ritter 1973, 3).

As the group develops in stages, the youngsters pass through dynamic periods of development. In the first half of the second year, which is considered the most quiet and most fruitful period of all, each individual arrives at a new self-evaluation. During this period of group formation, a new social consciousness is created. The adolescents have settled into a specific agricultural branch and are learning it thoroughly. In this last stage, they become interested in the current affairs of the kibbutz, while at school they are learning new subjects. Social activity is regulated and intense. As the group establishes bonds with youth movements in the country, the members become interested in local, national, social, and political questions. However, the group has not yet begun serious discussions about the future.

As the second year comes to a close, the future occupies the minds of the young people. Social activity reaches its zenith. Committee work is intense and increasingly independent. The *madrich* dares not press the youngsters into decisive discussions. He must allow them to arrive freely at the point of self-searching and decision. The number of youth that remain in the nucleus form a *garin*. In regard to Youth Aliyah's programs of the 1970s, the *garin* had as its goal to join the mother kibbutz after army service. As in the past, the ideology was based purely on the pioneering idea. After the two-year programs were completed, the nucleus group either remained a third year (working on the mother kibbutz), united with older *kibbutzim*, or lived in villages and worked as hired labor until the Jewish National Fund allotted them land on which to settle as an original *garin*. In time they joined a young kibbutz, which had not yet received its full complement of members. In the 1970s, however, the army period was divided between basic training, service in the kibbutz as part of the Israeli Army's *Nachal* Program, and the unique goal of returning to the kibbutz as members of the *garin* and the settlement itself.

Today, Youth Aliyah does not view as a failure other possibilities such as some of the graduates of the program joining a separate army unit from that of the *garin* and/or returning to their original neighborhoods, or any other rural or urban settlement other than the kibbutz. In this case, the goal of social integration has not necessarily replaced the long-range goal of the earlier period, but it clearly plays a more dominant role than the previous pioneering goals of the 1940s to 1960s.

The goal of the educational program at Ramat Hakovesh was explicitly to rehabilitate and prepare a group of disadvantaged Sephardic Jewish youth to be constructive citizens in society. The group was to be absorbed into the kibbutz in 1975 and remain there until 1977, when army service began. It was written and stated at various times that breaking the "welfare cycle" of the family and neighborhood, even if the subjects did not settle in the kibbutz after their army service, was the goal set by the Youth Aliyah supervisor, the *madrich*, the teacher, the housemother, the kibbutz members, and the social workers of the Tel Aviv municipality. From their point of view, success was achieved by the group that joined the *Nachal* and even considered remaining as a *garin* to Ramat Hakovesh after their army service was completed.

Recently, curricula for such peer group programs were developed by Dr. Belinda Biscoe, Carolyn Wakely, and John Mayfield of Oklahoma City. Before some of the contents of the curricula are outlined, it must be understood for whom a curriculum had been organized and how the developers envisaged that the techniques would help accomplish the goals of the agency that planned to use them. The leadership curriculum for ages thirteen to eighteen was used by counselors and volunteers to help teenagers build self-esteem and use personal power and knowledge to combat negative peer pressure situations, especially relating to the issues of drug and alcohol abuse by adolescents in the community zones chosen by A Chance for Youth. The grant to write the curriculum was given to Eagle Ridge, the organization that developed the five-year project of A Chance for Youth. The curriculum was printed, and A Chance for Youth then began to train counselors and volunteers with the monies given by the Office of Substance Abuse Prevention of the United States Department of Health and Human Services for use by agencies such as the Eagle Ridge Institute, to develop its community projects. As the project was established by the counselors of A Chance for Youth in 1992, the curriculum, which includes twenty-four sessions, was applied.

(It is included in Appendix I.) Some of the sessions were on peer
pressure, decision making, communicating feelings, drug and alcohol
information, a celebration of individual freedom, and feelings about self
and influences. Every session included goals and activities and, at times,
a quiz game and tips for the facilitator.   Each volunteer and counselor
was instructed   at workshops by the psychologist who wrote the
curriculum, with the assistance of other trained counselors who were
using the curriculum.

At a workshop session I attended as a volunteer, Dr. Biscoe asked me
to role-play a teenager being pressured to smoke marijuana by two peers.
I was to resist their offers as much as possible. After their three attempts
lasting ten minutes each, they did wear me down; but they were not able
to overcome my personal resistance. According to Dr. Biscoe, it was a
good simulation of the real thing. I did admit that under her direction my
resistance might have been overcome completely with an additional ten or
fifteen minutes of pressure. (For the reader's understanding, I have
included Session V on Peer Pressure in Appendix II, as well as Session
XVI on the Game Show Facts and Fiction on Drug and Alcohol Abuse
and Its Dangers in Appendix III.)

The Highfields New Jersey Project, a very successful peer group
program for juvenile delinquents in New Jersey, achieved goals that
eliminated the warehousing of juvenile delinquents. Its propositions
include the following:

1. The delinquent will change his or her behavior in a presocial direction
   only if his or her conduct change is acceptable to the peer group.
2. The change is meant to reach all in the group, and the directors believe
   it will be most effective if the change is aimed at the whole group.
3. Change itself will occur through a process of integration with others
   who are also undergoing change within the program.

By necessity, this program's success included a committed staff and the
support of the community in which it existed. The Highfields Project had
an environment that supported its noninstitutionalized program as it
developed in a particularly positive peer group mode.

As already mentioned, the directors of the Youth Aliyah Peer Group
Program, the Boys Town Ranch, and A Chance for Youth also knew that
those two variables must be included over a good number of years in
order to achieve success. It has been observed by educational researchers
that the lines of continuity from the 1970s Highfields New Jersey Project
for Juvenile Delinquents and the Youth Aliyah Rehabilitation programs in

Kibbutz (of the same decades of origins) were absorbed, to a large extent, by the newer programs of the late 1980s and early 1990s. The latter remain anti-institutionalization, peer group, and curriculum oriented and have been set up with the purpose of developing a highly supportive populace in the target community. In some cases, the community needed to be strengthened; and, in some cases, the two-year programs were established in already existing positive ideological environments.

In all of the aforementioned cases, a high percentage of at-risk youth have been or will soon be rehabilitated. Their newfound successes in school and at work will not be reversed later in life (i.e., that feared sociological term, *recidivism*, will not raise its ugly head). In these programs, the psychological freedom from both shame and negative reactions to society will play a major role in the overall educational rehabilitation process.

In that these alternative educational processes will be able to create real interest in learning; in that such peer group organized programs will provide stimulation that incorporates freedom and not suppressive discipline; and in that those programs will allow for normal tensions between self-governing student groups and adults who guide them, leading to more positive social relationships later in life, they will be more effective in their rehabilitation than the punishment mode for at-risk youth who lack the responsibility to organize their own lives during their stay in detention centers and overly structured group homes in this country. In most of those institutions, only control and discipline reign, not freedom and not the necessary peer group work that creates interest and desire to learn and develop positive relationships now and in the future.

Chapter 2

Modern Peer Group Ideas: To What Extent Will They Succeed to Integrate At-Risk Youth?

> When a child cannot get love, he will ask for hate in abundance.
>
> A. S. Neill

In a wonderful little book, *Letters to a Teacher* (Rossi and Cole 1971) by the school boys of Barbiani (in Italy), the recruitment into the school of two at-risk youth was described in such a way that it reminded me of A. S. Neill's famous progressive school, Summerhill. In fact, much of the rest of the school's philosophy did as well, including the role that a teacher should play and how the school should be governed. Consider the following excerpt:

Sandro was fifteen, five feet in height, a humiliated adult. His teachers had declared him an imbecile. They expected him to repeat the first intermediate for the third time. Gianni was fourteen. Inattentive, allergic to reading, his teachers had declared him a delinquent. They were not totally wrong, but that was no excuse for sweeping him out of the way. Neither of them had any intention of repeating. *They had reached the point of dropping out and getting jobs.* (my italics)

They came over to us because we ignore your failing marks and put each person in the right grade for his age. Sandro was put in the third intermediate and Gianni in the second. This was the first satisfaction they ever had in their careers. Sandro will remember this forever. Gianni remembers once in a while. (Rossi and Cole 1971, 10)

Later in the book, under a subheading "Sovereignty," the eight schoolboy authors wrote, "Let us try to educate our children to a higher ambition. To become sovereigns. Forget about doctor or engineer" (Rossi and Cole 1971, 91). In this school, peer group organization was evident. "To think about it at great length. To have friends help us in patient teamwork" (Rossi and Cole 1971, 127). Although the school disbanded when its principal, an ordained priest, died in 1967, its little farming town building remained a meeting place for the students for years after. They had already become technicians, industrial laborers, or student teachers by the mid-1970s. However, it is not only their career outcomes that prove that such teamwork or peer group cooperation can be a successful method for educating poor urban or rural children who are failing inside and outside school, but also the methods by which they had worked as a team to write their book: first pooling all their thoughts and then trimming them into plain speaking language. This is what can convince a reader about the positive results of a real peer group approach in a school for failing youth.

This group is a model for other at-risk youth who need to cut through the accumulations of nonsense and let out the truth about their feelings and ideas about their world. What can hinder modern teachers from facilitating such learning? Another phrase which especially struck a chord was in regard to the connection between peer group programming and how high-risk youth can have pride in their school work. It dealt with writing as an art. "And don't say that you lack the time for it. It would be enough to have one long paper written throughout the year, but written by all students together" (Rossi and Cole 1971, 122).

Community centers in urban environments can use that model, as can many schools in dire straits with regard to the number of at-risk youth who attend. In Pittsburgh, Castle on the Hill, a project at Fort Pitt Elementary School, included a method whereby children wrote and illustrated their own books as well as learned procedures to publish them. In April 1993, I also read a Pittsburgh newspaper "designed by and for teenagers," *Sign of the Times*, which has been available in Pittsburgh's Kingsley House Community Center since 1989. These are only two examples designed to develop independent sovereign youth who learn by making choices and working together as a team.

In my own classrooms, it soon became evident to me that all of the acting-out students in the 1992/93 school year could become artists, writers, or engineers if they could get beyond themselves by creating historical or cultural projects as a team. Those boys and girls did cooperate and develop their own building techniques a number of times that year. I saw my role as trying quietly to facilitate the projects by providing students with resources and time. Many students believe that tests and exams are a waste of time (e.g., sixty days out of two hundred and ten days wasted in Barbiani). In an attack on their teachers, one of the schoolboys wrote, "While giving a test, you used to walk up and down between the rows of desks and see me in trouble and making mistakes, but you never said a word. I have the same situation at home. No one to turn to for help for miles around" (Rossi and Cole 1971, 122).

At Summerhill and Barbiani, the teacher's role was to facilitate intellectual learning and a socialization process, a dual concept that our schools need to absorb in the 1990s. In this way, youth with low self-esteem would develop pride and react positively to the reality they will enter after leaving school.

During Neill's first year of international school experience, he admired Professor Zutt who was an artist-craftsperson. Zutt's aim in teaching handiwork was to help children experience the joy of creation of which all were capable if given the opportunity to make what they wanted and learn techniques as they created, unrestrained by practice exercises. "What Zutt calls FREUDE (joy), I call interest," Neill writes, "and although our terms are different we are completely at one in our attitude to education" (Neill 1960, 159). It is incumbent on me to add that in Summerhill, the dual concept was evident in the overall philosophy of community. In *Children's Freedom: A. S. Neill and the Evolution of the Summerhill Idea*, Ray Hemmings directs the reader's attention to two ideas: "Interactions within the school community is one of the most important sources of learning . . . , and there is a definite attempt to articulate the communal will and the various individual wills, and to find a workable balance" (Hemmings 1973, 188). In many ways, the children and adults enjoyed equality. At the minimum, there were equal voting rights at decision-making meetings, except in areas in which students' physical well-being was concerned. The teacher had to relate to the children in the context of his or her expertise and resources, but it is a reciprocal relationship; and the children's various resources and their expertise are as significant an ingredient in the interaction as the teacher's (Hemmings 1973, 192). As one of Neill's major mentors had said, "self-government is the personal responsibility of the individual for the social worth of the community" (Willis 1960, 90).

Learning and socialization occurred simultaneously, and it is no wonder that Summerhill was the most progressive model in British schools for many years. It was certainly the most successful. Educators such as John

Holt, Robert Coles, Ray Hemmings, Pablo Friere, and Jonathan Kozol have lauded it either directly or by expressing their own ideas and wishes to love and rehabilitate troubled children and communities.

Summerhill astonished parents and teachers around the world. *Letters to a Teacher* was also for parents and teachers. Although Summerhill started out as an experimental school, it became a demonstration school. One has only to read the Foreword of *Summerhill*, written by Erich Fromm, the author of *Escape from Freedom*, to understand that Summerhill offered a humanistic education, not a religious one, and an education that included both intellectual and emotional growth for children in whom Neill had firm faith. Neill did believe in freedom but freedom to learn did not mean license, *and respect for the individual must be mutual*. The individual must not use force against others, but must learn to face life intellectually, emotionally, and artistically. In truth, Fromm found Neill to be a courageous person who faced reality as he saw it, and his school developed those goals for his students (Neill 1960, V-XVII).

In regard to the key concept of community, it had become obvious to the administrators of Youth Aliyah and, twenty years later, to the initiators of A Chance for Youth that only a very supportive group of families as volunteers and a totally positive approach by the kibbutz as a community could enable peer group programs to succeed. The counselors at A Chance for Youth had penetrated the community to a degree, but had not yet reached their main goals by 1992. The community of kibbutz, which had once agreed to be a sponsor, was a ready-made, idealistic, integrating community for at-risk youth. At Kibbutz Ramat Hakovesh, the social integration of many of the youth was pointed out to me by social worker, Aaron Sharon, who said that the nineteen youth were truly adopted by the families; that their participation in day-to-day kibbutz activities became normal procedure; and that the relationships that developed at work and with the equivalent-aged youth of the kibbutz were major factors in their integration in the kibbutz (Frank 1992, 50).

A Chance for Youth has a more difficult task than Youth Aliyah rehabilitation programs in kibbutz because the former lacks such a ready-made ideological community. It had to organize in advance to find churches and various community centers to act as bases for its programs with high-risk youth. After volunteer educators, myself included, were recruited to circulate in the poverty zone areas of Oklahoma City in order to find willing clergy or social workers who would open community center doors, A Chance for Youth began to recruit volunteers within the neighborhoods in which it had already begun to work with youth from seven to seventeen. In one of those neighborhoods where there had been much vandalism, recruiting volunteers led to a lessening of thefts in the neighborhood's business section. The counselors knew that those volunteers who had arrived to help had rapidly made the difference. I personally met many Hispanic, African American, and Native American volunteers at workshops sponsored by A Chance for Youth. They, too, would certainly make a difference. The long-range goal of such efforts was the eventual administration of programs by community volunteers with regular training sessions by A Chance for Youth. Because these neighborhood people were much poorer than the middle-class kibbutz sponsors, it is obvious that it would take four or five years to see success by volunteers and a sprinkling of staff, compared to Youth Aliyah's two-year programs that had achieved their rehabilitation goals. However, the small number of volunteers would eventually succeed, as a few examples have already shown.

In those poverty zones, one or two successes by volunteers will lead to more volunteers signing up, breeding further success with at-risk youth. Many volunteers will then convince neighbors and friends to join them. By 1992, minority groups in Oklahoma City had gained more power on the local Board of Education. Cooperation between public school officials and community organizations could enhance the ability of unique peer group programs to receive the necessary support in the poverty zones.

As more stress is given to skills, cultural consciousness, and pride within the school systems, community-based, nonformal social programs will be able to enhance simultaneously the economic development and socialization process of the neighborhood youth. It will be possible to organize special cultural programs for minority urban youth as well. Eagle Ridge, the social agency that sponsored A Chance for Youth, had already begun to do that by 1991 for Hispanic youth in Oklahoma. This idea to build pride has since spread to Texas, Louisiana, Arkansas, and California.

In 1976, reformers felt that the small free schools for the poor could only save a small number of the disadvantaged youth who had failed or were unhappy in the public schools; and that one danger was, as is with many reforms, that those nonformal learning environments would blunt the discontent before the public schools could bring about larger changes (Fanfani 1976, 84). We now know that this fear can be overcome with excellent counseling and educational work within supportive environments--the communities of Edmond, Oklahoma, for example, where the Boys Town Ranch exists. The Boys Town Ranch was able to teach academic and social skills to at-risk youth and integrate them into a middle-class community which was only a short ride away.

A Chance for Youth's experiment had already made great progress in poor communities, and the Youth Aliyah Peer Group programs in Kibbutz have been succeeding for twenty years in the idealistic kibbutz communities since the State of Israel lent its political and financial backing to the collectives and their ideological systems into which high-risk youth were absorbed. Such criticism as noted earlier could not have been farsighted enough to understand that the solutions were not in schools, but in the communities where youth lived for extended periods of time. In the 1990s, this type of community life alongside peer group programming should become the mode for rehabilitating at-risk youth. At the same time while A Chance for Youth was making inroads into poor Oklahoma City communities, a unique program just got off the ground in Houston, Texas and a detention center without bars in Montgomery County, Pennsylvania had proven its mettle in an advanced anti-warehousing program for juvenile delinquents.   Although it was a preparatory program for longer term rehabilitative social programs, the Montgomery County program had similarities to the Highfields, New Jersey Work Program and the Youth Aliyah *Kelet*. Its activities were field trips, classroom learning, counseling sessions, and sports on fields without bars and guards anywhere. Not only was that restriction missing, but the program's location in a residential area next to a country club was a suspect issue at the program's onset.

In Houston, Janice Hill initiated a peer group program in the Alief area of town. Although her two-year crusade was initiated to stem gang activity, it soon grew into a cultural awareness program which was a unique community effort. Hill and other volunteers organized evening activities, classes, and rap sessions to break through to kids who were heading nowhere.   In May 1991, plans were being made to open a community center with a nonprofit status. In her honest way, Hill said that she did not expect to turn a child who was on the wrong path into an angel overnight, but kids could be kept off the streets and given something constructive to do.

In a discussion with my own classes in 1993, the ability to get decent jobs after school or household chores to earn money, as well as being involved in community activities which were not gang related, appealed to students. This was also the expectation they held if the solutions to the problems of many of their peers were to be found. In many communities such as theirs, the police were considered the enemy, since their initial approaches were filled with threats of force, not positive assistance (which could co-opt youth in the neighborhood). For example, most Pittsburgh teenagers with whom I spoke believed that their community had a better chance to succeed than the police force of Pittsburgh.

In some cities and large counties where there is an increasing amount of violence in public schools and nearby areas, even rural so-called environmental ranch-type programs that have been used to solve the delinquent difficulties have not succeeded when staff have acted like a private police force. Although the Pennsylvania State Education Association (P.S.E.A.) reported more violence in the schools in Allegheny County, a Washington County youth farm found that its staff was being accused of hitting children. Recently, it decided to become a private institution (Jones 1994, b1; Lee 1994, b7).

The techniques that good peer group programs have used include: information giving; sensitivity exercises with organized groups; mediation; mentors; volunteer tutors who work with groups together or individually; and activities organized by well trained counselors, many of whom have been abused or who have had substance abuse problems themselves. Of course, the most caring teachers and psychologists also create pride, not shame, in youngsters. As mentioned in Chapter 1, special exercises have been developed for youth in the unique peer group programs. Many of those adolescents already have been addicted to drugs and alcohol. Some at-risk youth also need help in understanding how drugs impact society and families. Therefore, I have included in Appendix IV two good examples that have been used in Eagle Ridge (A Chance for Youth). By receiving important information through exercises and well developed videos, both the eight- to twelve-year-old and the thirteen- to eighteen-year old groups have been prevented from joining in gang violence related to drug and alcohol abuse. The other exercises developed by psychologists from Eagle Ridge have created a totally successful program, according to A Chance for Youth counselors and psychologists. In my interviews with them, the major response to my question, "Can you document positive results because of your peer group programs with younger groups (ages eight to thirteen) and even some older youth from poverty zones in South Oklahoma City and cities in Texas as well?" was always, "Yes, we can document such success if we use a holistic approach and work with parents, judges, detention center staff, teachers, and counselors. We must give all those people the tools to work with. We must not blame them, as most Americans have done in the past." This statement was meant to emphasize that they could not constantly blame the parents.

Another peer group program that has used a holistic approach is Orr Shalom in Jerusalem. Orr Shalom was a pioneer, one of the first therapeutic family group homes in Israel for deprived, abused, and neglected children. Each home has eight to ten children (including the children of the house parents) who are supervised and trained by Orr Shalom's professional staff, which consists of social workers and psychologists. Children are encouraged to interact within the community where they live. They participate in local youth groups and activities at neighborhood community centers (drama, football, judo, field trips). In a letter dated October 1991, Orr Shalom's assistant director described a new internship program through which the children were hired to work in many places, such as a hair salon, an office of the Ministry of Education, and a grocery store. The children also volunteered at a senior citizens' home; and, in a newsletter, it was emphasized how two or three girls from the program had developed close relationships with the residents of the senior citizens' home.

Before describing individual work with at-risk youth, we must discuss the dynamics of gangs or peer groups, which have created new problems for our cities and for youth. What approach can help solve those problems or at least point to a new direction? First, gang members need to be identified. Who are they? They are peer group members who are seeking answers to their own questions: "Who am I and what am I going to be?" The banding together allows them to solve status issues. By threatening violence and dabbling in illegal activities, they can solve their economic problems, at least until they get incarcerated or are killed because they intruded on another gang's territory. Smaller cities are trying to deal with the problems of gang members by involving social workers, community police, volunteer tutors, staff of YMCAs, and church leaders to make as many one-on-one contacts as possible with teenagers. Movies and rap music glorified gangs, and smaller cities (under 500,000 in population) were penetrated in the late 1980s by drug dealers. Many of the traditional organizations, such as the YMCA or street ministries, do not talk to the media now for fear of appearing to be antigang. However, they know that job searches, counseling in groups, and sports activities-- not highly visible suppressive police action--have a much higher success rate in achieving gang members' peaceful socialization.

The monstrous gangs in Los Angeles, Detroit, and Chicago have grown so large because police suppression and punishment were used as the means, not individual and group socialization and economic betterment processes. In smaller cities, the holistic approach with groups and individuals will lead to more positive results. This is what psychologists and counselors in the Southwest and small midwestern cities have already learned from their own experiences. How long will it take the eastern and larger cities in the Midwest to grasp those same ideas?

Chapter 3

Counseling and Caring: How Individual Psychologists, Counselors, Teachers, and Volunteers Can Intervene with At-Risk Youth

As teachers, psychologists, social workers, or mentors, all of us have known either a few or even many special at-risk children. Some educators have tried to guide and help those few, tens, or even hundreds of such young people. I have seen or heard about the successes of those adults with high-risk youth. In more recent times, I have also had some influence on or have guided a few children, helping them resist the pressures that usually lead to danger and failure, eventually to develop into resilient citizens, students, workers, and good family members. Psychologists have their own stories to relate. Several are included in this chapter and others are chronicled in such books as *Building Self-Esteem in Children* (Berne and Savary 1987). None of the success stories make the headlines in our local newspapers; therefore, I have chosen to relate a few of them in this chapter. All of them are about high-risk youth of the 1980s and 1990s. To retain confidentiality, the names and initials have been changed.

On Friday in 1984, I was taking a break in the small kitchen of a Three Rivers Youth building in which the Pittsburgh Alternative Educational Vocation Program (A.E.V.P.) was housed. That unique program began in November 1983. Suddenly, K. walked in and asked me if he could wash my car. He was twenty years old and on probation. K. started to wash and polish my car that day; however, he did not finish the job that Friday but offered to return the following week. He eventually washed my car twice and polished it as well; but before he completed the work, he caused me a great deal of anxiety. He and my 1976 Ford disappeared for a few hours. He told me that he had returned to his Northview Heights neighborhood to find some rags, and it took him a little longer than he thought it would to travel that short distance.

K. progressed through our program and developed enough trust in us to stay in September and earn an unofficial completion certificate. Whatever success we had in communicating with him, building his trust in us, and raising his self-esteem had influenced him to become part of us and our program.

Six years later, in 1990, I was a principal of a religious school. One student, C., was continually teased by other students for her inability to understand the Hebrew language. C. also felt that her family, who had adopted her at an early age, had not always loved her. She periodically sought out her real mother. C. acted out a great deal and was accused of stealing a watch. The following year began with more positive signs. C. was learning better and her attitude had improved. However, after several months, her behavior once again became inappropriate, despite the caring efforts of her teachers. The educational committee understood that she had a behavioral disorder and agreed to my suggestion that I tutor C. on a one-on-one basis for four hours a week, while at the same time beginning preparation toward her Bat Mitzvah. For the next several months, C. and I developed a trusting relationship. We also worked diligently on her Hebrew language skills so that she would feel confident with her peers with whom she had not previously related well. I also gave her a different pen every week, since she had admired each one that I used during her tutoring sessions. We bonded well; and as she progressed in her studies and received praise from me and some of her classmates, she exhibited more confidence. Then, that illusive self-esteem began to emerge and her overall class behavior improved. Success did breed success.

Although she was very nervous on the special day when she became a Bat Mitzvah, C. actually read, sang, and spoke very well; and, in a spiritual way, she rose above her classmates. Our communication continued into 1993 even though she was in Oklahoma City while I had returned to Pittsburgh. Although a family tragedy created a difficult obstacle for C., she continued to do well in school. As late as May 1993, the feedback concerning C. was positive, both from the Rabbi and her mother. This resilient young lady was succeeding beyond expectations, even though it continued to be a struggle for her.

At-risk youth are starving for care and attention. With honest and generous doses of praise and by being positive role models, the caring teachers of America have influenced many troubled young people. Children who vent anger because of shame, embarrassment, or despair, need help from everyone. It is obvious that the Vs. and Ts. who curse, who constantly ask about their grades, and who try to win awards and are ecstatic if they win only one, are numerous in our urban schools today. Nothing can be taken for granted. If only one of them told me that he or she loved me and another wrote that he or she came to like me better, I honestly marvel at the connection that can be made in six months of a school year, during which time those at-risk youth were in my class.

T. never liked to go to the library to do class projects. She once wrote her nickname on a table, cursed at the librarian who asked her to remove it, and refused to apologize, even after the parent came in to discuss her behavior. As one of eight children, T. obviously was clawing her way through life. As her teacher, I praised her, smiled at her, and reminded her of what was appropriate and inappropriate behavior. I also spoke to T. about confrontations and the art of diplomacy. Eventually, T. stopped cursing and began participating and contributing even in the library. My final reward was what T. had written on my evaluation sheet: "I got to like you better."

V. never achieved scholastically in the advanced classes and had some serious difficulties in controlling her behavior in and out of school. However, in six months (albeit with some ups and downs, especially during those last hot days in June) she became an A student, even winning the Student of the Month award in the spring. I realized that all I did was recognize her learning attempts, periodically praise her achievement, give her one reward, and try to find her an after-school job. Not much extra effort on my part, but what a difference to her. And I was rewarded with: "I love you, Dr. Frank," as V. stated in class, not once but twice. Most veteran educators have never heard such words during their careers. Finally, I began to understand that it was more in V.'s makeup to express her feelings towards me than it was in mine to receive such expressions of emotion comfortably.

When T. wrote on my evaluation sheet that she came to like me better, I understood that my hard work and guidance, not leading and doing the work for her, had finally clicked in terms of her actually making a positive connection with me. The day before the class history final, T. came up to me in the hall to say, "Good bye" and to tell me that she was leaving for Philadelphia that day. We both smiled and said, "Good bye." I told her that I would miss her. We had expressed our mutual appreciation;

and although she would not be in school next year, another successful relationship had been built. Once that hard shell had been broken and a difficult personality had been moderated, a more mature, sociable, and resilient young lady could face the world.

The troubled, tempestuous exteriors of students like T., V., and C. can be broken through and overcome by nurturing teachers. The great efforts made by psychologists, counselors, government job initiators, librarians, and community leaders who promote business and recreational centers for youth in our urban neighborhoods are also essential. Of course, long-range educational programs and facilities in communities need to be developed with state and federal grants. The ingredient of volunteer and professionally staffed programs such as A Chance for Youth is a key to the rehabilitation of high-risk youth. Otherwise, the desperate situation in which many of our youth find themselves will continue to exist.

One of the best mentors I ever met in the field not only worked with a few youth from an alternative school, but also found time to organize his own mentoring organization, Forward Oklahoma. Since he was my neighbor for two years, I observed his work firsthand and also became a mentor to a thirteen-year-old, H. who had just entered the program.   H. and I played basketball and went to professional games. I checked on his homework once a week and stayed in touch with the principal of his alternative public school. The program helped him transfer to a regular public school in his own neighborhood in the spring of 1992. Eventually my neighbor, Wade, made connections with the local YMCA and YWCA and other social agencies so that he could recruit and train other mentors. This was the first experience that Wade had in either education or social work with children who had problems. Wade's enthusiasm led to the successes of bank employees and many other nonprofessional tutors and mentors in 1992 and 1993. Oklahoma City was fortunate to have a caring businessman such as Wade who helped adult volunteers become role models for at-risk youth.

The following story of resilience and independence was told to me by Belinda Biscoe in October 1994. It is a story to which I will refer again in Chapter 6 as well as in this chapter. All of the cases related in Chapter 6 and in this chapter will be stories of psychologists, student teachers, or high school teachers, all of whom work with high-risk youth.

The young person called X. was in trouble for a juvenile crime when Belinda began to work with him through a court organized program in which Belinda was directly involved. Belinda counseled X. and helped him get a part-time job. While X. was on probation, he called Belinda once a month or more, and she learned about his youth, including his family problems (which included being sexually abused at the age of seven). X. finally made it to his final semester in high school. That year he called Belinda on Mother's Day, since both of his parents were not in the picture and he was living with an aunt. There were many other times that X. called his new role model who also acted as his surrogate mother. Such times were when he had problems on the job or needed help to develop other strategies. Finally, X. was released from the court's jurisdiction and he immediately called Belinda to tell her this. When she screamed her congratulations on the phone and told him she was ecstatic, X. was quiet for a minute and then practically screamed back to Belinda, "Does that mean I am out of your program, too?" He had been so resilient and had overcome his background problems, as well as all his issues with the court, and now he was afraid to lose his one role model. In effect, X. had independently recruited Belinda as a role model and had progressed. Now he would not lose her. Belinda told me that this was not an unusual story. Many young people do this some of the time. It would be more unusual if it did not happen.

In the literature I have read about building self-esteem in youth, one book, *Building Self-Esteem in Children* (Berne and Savary 1987), stands out in my mind. This book includes the best down-to-earth methods that I have read or seen in ten years. One example related in the book is the story of A. A. was a second grader ostensibly sent to Patricia for tutoring. In reality, A. was considered a problem child by her teachers and classmates, "bossy, selfish, uncooperative, and given to tantrums." However, Patricia never experienced those negative qualities with A. during the year because all those characteristics were channeled through A.'s creative energy.

A booklet was turned in, gift-wrapped, tied with a ribbon, and addressed to Patricia. Projects such as this one, usually with a drawing on the cover and a one- or two-page story inside, were created and completed by A. as "gifts" for Patricia who acknowledged them over and over throughout the year. A.'s bossiness found its outlet when A. invited classmates to Patricia's office at lunch time and led them in short productions of her own creativity. Patricia became the one-person captive audience. She then rewarded A. and her classmates with candies from a bag which Patricia kept in her desk for such occasions.

A.'s relationships with her peers were steadily improving; and this process culminated in her organizing, with six classmates, a surprise birthday party for Patricia. A. had received social cooperation from her classmates by giving them the candy she received from Patricia for reading sentences correctly. What Patricia Berne had done was destroy the destructive cycle by developing a cycle that nourished A.'s self-esteem.

Peer leaders who show signs of being positive need to be given the correct guidance to allow them to lead other youth down the right path. For example, I watched D. lead his peers in class and then one day I noticed his name, along with the names of four other boys from the tenth and eleventh grades, on a list to meet with a young black male security person who represented the administration. The picture of positive attempts by the administration to develop peer leaders suddenly flashed through my mind. I had openly been trying to develop such peer leaders in my own class, and D. had fit into that effort after only three or four months.

D. seldom acted out in class, and he tried to focus on the subject of the day although his attention span lasted for only the first thirty or forty minutes of our fifty-minute class. We talked often about athletes, as he was talented, but too small to become a professional football player. He already recognized that his goal had to be to improve his academic skills in order to take advantage of his potential football scholarship to a small college. His ability to overcome negative peer pressures led many teachers to encourage, help, and love him; he was helping many of his peers at the same time.

A great football coach, Pete Dimperio, at George Westinghouse High School in Pittsburgh, Pennsylvania had chosen youth such as D. to be leaders on the great football teams of the 1950s. These youth not only became football team leaders but, for many years, were positive school leaders as well. Pete, Jr. told me in the summer of 1993 that it was on the strong arms and legs of such youth that positive peer groups and good school years were built at George Westinghouse High.

K. was a young man whose father was often away from home and whose mother, as I later learned, was in Florida, as was K.'s girlfriend. Late in June, K. told me that he had an upcoming trial in Pittsburgh; and if it worked out okay, he was going to return to Florida. Another teacher also told me that K. had allegedly broken the law in Maryland. K. was sixteen, cursed often in class, was extremely loud, teased other boys, and acted roughly (usually with a smile on his face so that his peers would not take him too seriously). I found him a job in the nice business area of my upper middle-class community. He soon moved to a five-day-a-week af-ter-school job in the same block and attended classes regularly during the fourth report period. He started to study and do all the class assignments.

Almost every day during the last few minutes of class, K., several other students, and I would have a brief job club discussion. The influence of these regular class attendees, as well as A and B students who also got involved, carried over to other boys and girls who did not have good attendance.

By May 1993, K.'s attitude and behavior in class became positive. By May 1993, his pride was evident; and his self-esteem factor rose by at least 100 points. By June, he knew that he had become an A student in World Cultures and I learned that he was also doing well in English. During the last report period, K. received an E grade from me because his attendance was extremely poor. His final grade of C gave him a big lift, and I knew from his smile that his A was the *coup de grace* of the year for K. On the last day of school, K. left the classroom saying, "I am going to Florida soon and will not see you next year, Dr. Frank." He was straight and solemn in his expression. We then shook hands, and I wished him well in his new environment with his mother. I honestly felt, and told him so, that he had found some assurance that he could do well in, as well as outside of, school. I was elated that I had helped this juvenile, who had brushed with the negative aspects of society, now act as though he saw the chance to be a positive person in the future. K. confirmed what I told him by nodding his head, smiling, and saying good bye again. This was not the same acting-out, aggressive, angry juvenile delinquent whom I had met in December 1992.

In the last three months, I had often met L. on the streets of my community. He was looking for a job. He had always been friendly and fun loving in class, but his behavior had also created some difficulties for me as his World Cultures teacher. I never guessed that I could find him a job in March, but I did. By July, he would be earning $350 a month, working several days a week. This money, he told me, was to help his mother. He had been teased by his friends on the baseball team because I had driven him to his first and only job interview. In the school hallways and on the athletic field, his peers referred to me as his dad; yet there was some sense of envy mingled with the good natured teasing. Later, I noticed that if a student was offensive to me, L. quickly, but quietly, corrected that student. In March 1993, L. was only fifteen, mischievous yet pleasant, sometimes angry and tough, but also very skilled in academics and especially in art projects. L. was able to charm adults quite easily, and in the nomenclature he was referred to as a "Hooker."

L.'s grades should have been in the B range. However, he was still immature and did not possess enough self-confidence to be consistent. I spent ten months attempting to get him to focus more on school work and less on gang mottoes and writings. I believe that his talent, the job, and my demonstrative concern helped L. get through the school year with a C average. I tried to bridge the gap between his life in the dangerous ghetto and a more positive world. His becoming more involved in work and school created the extra needed resilience for an already good person. I hope that someday he will handle reality in the most constructive ways he can, which will lead him to attain positive results in society.

A friend of mine who has worked for many years with at-risk adolescents recently told me the following story: Z. was a sixteen-year-old male who came to an open house of a social agency where my friend was working. Z.'s background was troublesome; his father's whereabouts were unknown and his mother was in jail on drug charges. Z. was admitted to our program. His test results proved him to be very bright. Z. studied hard, received his GED diploma, and was being considered for admission to a community college. One June day, a probation officer came to the program's facility to check on another student. The officer noticed Z. and told the coordinator that Z. had run away from a detention center and had been adjudicated only two months before his program there ended. After some discussion, Z. made his own decision to turn himself in to the detention center. Although the judge was told that Z. had been doing constructive work in the program and should not be readjudicated to serve time, Z. was forced to spend that lost time at the detention center. When Z. returned to his home, he began to look for work and to help his mother become healthy. My friend visited Z. in the detention center and is still in touch with him to advise him of job possibilities. In 1993, she told me that Z. had never again given in to the wrong crowd, had never again committed a crime, and that he tried to stay on the right side of the law. The odds are now fifty-fifty that Z. will be within society's rules and outside the circles of crime. This was partly because of one person's caring and continual concern.

Chapter 4 will be an extension of the success stories recounted in this chapter. Although the stories of youth aged thirteen to twenty-five include positive changes, the caring adults could only create the methods and give the attention necessary to temporarily solve some of the problems of the children who lacked any resilience. The stories of children and youth who have actually advanced to positive leadership roles as good citizens must also be added before this book can be complete.

Chapter 4

Meaningful Events in the Lives of Professionals: Helping At-Risk Youth Be Free to Learn and Succeed

From 1979 to 1991, fifty thousand teenagers were killed by guns--as many U.S. lives that were lost in the Vietnam War. In 1993, when homicides in Pittsburgh broke an all-time record that was set in 1917; in a year when the Secretary of Education, Riley, felt the need to plead with parents to "slow down the pace of their lives to help children"; in a year when at least 1,000 people in Pittsburgh marched for nonviolence in a city neighborhood racked by homicides; and in a year when hundreds had marched earlier in another dangerous part of Pittsburgh and another group was attacking the enemy on corners where drug dealing and violence regularly occurred, we finally began to understand how parents, teachers, social workers, counselors, average citizens, and community-oriented police must cooperate to prevent the need to warehouse those youth who were not yet in jail and who had not yet joined the gangs; that is, succumbed to the peer pressures that could destroy them.

As one outreach counselor in Pittsburgh recently said to teachers, "Ninety percent of our youth are not in gangs; but neither the stars, the educators, nor the counselors themselves has delivered the right up-to-date messages to a majority of our poor youth. Hip Hop Rap has been their TV," he said. Peer pressures not only drew them into sexual activities, but drugs and crime became their new masters of rebellion.

More poor children are involved in those activities since the rage and despair have not been heard by our educational establishment, our government, and the wealthy citizens of our business community. From this perspective, all youth at risk--white, black, or Hispanic--have suffered the same neglect. Since American youth in the 1990s are constantly moving targets, the authentic messages delivered by some caring people have not reached them. Rap, however, tells them what exactly is happening, and one can hear and see this if one observes that audiences absorb those messages and receive the sanction that allows their at-risk attitudes to manifest themselves in illegal and dangerous ways. Their new creative goal is to write their own rap, and this is being done every day of the week in our schools.

Although there are interracial gangs, youth in black ghettos openly say to counselors and some teachers, "This is a white country."; "Christmas is a white man's holiday."; and "I hope that there is no white snow on Christmas." I have personally heard a number of these statements. Thus, I have learned firsthand that the racist element in them is an expression of despair and rage, especially when it comes at holiday times alongside statements like, "I do not care about Christmas: No one is buying me a present anyhow." One young student recently told me that children at his school cannot mix racially for fear of being attacked by racial gangs or a few individuals of their own race who were ready to hurt them if they tried to mix.

For all of our attempts to work with such at-risk youth, many adults still assume that they cannot help more than a few children at a time. However, with better communication, creativity, and good programming established for parents and youth; with the training of more professionals; and by utilizing community facilities, churches, community centers, and playgrounds for recreation, we could provide resilience to much larger numbers of our young people, thus building the new programs and making more contributions toward helping them reach their inherent goals. Both professionals and business leaders, as well as parents, and neighbors, need to begin to be part of the special efforts of long-range alternative programs if progress in poorer communities will ever occur.

Programs such as A Chance for Youth and other long-range alternative educational programs in supportive environments already have set models. So have schools such as Summerhill; Youth Aliyah's Rehabilitation programs in Israeli *Kibbutzim*; the Boys Town Ranch in Norman, Oklahoma; and Kozol's Free Schools. There are not any good educational reasons why such programs and schools cannot be replicated in the 1990s to reach more children who are at risk. Otherwise, only a handful of young people can be helped in each community by some teachers, counselors, principals, and volunteers who care enough to reach out to our youth.

Some of the teachers, psychologists, and counselors whom I have met in the last few years have reached out often, even though they have not felt entirely successful. Some of these people have given up, but some continue to try to help as many at-risk youth as possible. When they have given up, it is mainly because cooperation with some bureaucrat of the labor department or funds from local administrators cannot be attained.

There are many kinds of youth who talk to me in school or indirectly relate their stories to me through intermediaries; i.e., counselors or other teachers or even friends. They say things such as: "I'm hungry."; "Gangs push so much."; "One of my boys was shot."; "Prison may be my only choice."; "Why work for $500 a week if I can make $500 a day?"; "White people look scared when we walk into their neighborhood."; and "I miss M. " (someone who was recently killed).

Some teenagers do take ownership and responsibility if they lose control (e.g., apologizing for cursing). Some also decide to try to learn, graduate, and leave the ghetto life behind them. When some teenagers role-play (e.g., a girl who role-played a union steward in a 1912 sweatshop), they wear a mask that enables them to transcend acting-out behavior. In fact, the girl in the aforementioned role play did not risk anything. She became a union leader--a smart one at that--during class time. Later, she began to work and learned about wages, working conditions, and union benefits in 1993-1994 in class and on the job.

There are those youth who do not even consider the idea of being re-sponsible for their words or actions since their rage usually overwhelms them. Suddenly, banging his book on the table when he thinks of some-thing, A. displays his anger. This is not unusual. I have asked him and others what is wrong or what happened and their response is a shrug. There are other children who are hungry and do not consider free school breakfasts adequate. If they do talk openly about their hunger, the teacher can offer them a good apple turnover from a food service department dur-ing lunch, and they will often accept it. Usually they are too shy to walk over to that department to request the turnover even if it is free to them. (I usually remind them to do so if I see them in the hallway near noon time.) It is easy for my students and thousands of others like them to see how they have been victims of the system, and how they are in the system mainly because people at home do not care or have not cared. I have met many youth who are in the juvenile justice system, and they are sad and angry.

At times, hunger, spiritual pain, low self-esteem, and a lack of confidence in their future can easily lead such youth to gang life--"the set." Hundreds of youth have no other adults or place to turn to for support. In Pittsburgh, Pennsylvania, on February 11, 1994, the Commission on Human Relations listened to students between the ages of nine and twenty who discussed the wish list of inner city youth:

1. More nurturing and discipline at home
2. More support and respect from adults in their schools and communities
3. More exposure to mentors and role models
4. More year-round jobs
5. More funding for after-school and community educational and recreational programs
6. More communication and cooperation among those trying to address drugs, violence, and other problems affecting young people.

One young girl said she was one of eight children who grew up in group and foster homes. "She almost fell into the same pitfalls as many wayward children but found self-esteem" by attending a good private school. Her final statement, quoted in the *Pittsburgh Post-Gazette*, was, "I came here to tell you my story, my pain, my sorrows can be another person's fortune" (Jones 1994, A12).

One angry-looking student was coming to my history class regularly in 1993, and a colleague told me that the young person trusted me. I never screamed at him, and I tried very hard every day to get him started on his classwork. Although he did his classwork only 25 to 30 percent of the time, it was gratifying to watch him moderate his behavior in class and participate at times, as well. Even if he just sat quietly and listened, a partial success was evident. In late December, there was an altercation with a vice principal, and the student was suspended for a number of days. Then he missed a few more days, and I did not see him at all until early January. It is important for teachers to work with such young people in the classroom, but it is even more important to reach them as human beings. Although I had seen flashes of the student's anger once or twice in my class, I would rather it occur there occasionally than not see him for many days at a time. He worked very hard and at the end of the first semester, he earned a C grade. A. S. Neill would have been more interested in the student's well-being than in his academic performance; and later on that year, this student's psychological well-being became my priority.

In the last few years, I have begun to comprehend as a teacher that my most difficult and most interesting students are not objects to be controlled but people to be reached in a spiritual sense. Once that happens, then there is the chance to help students be creative and constructive members of the classroom. Such efforts can lead to the academic and social development of many youth so they can be positive people in their communities and in a stronger society which learns to celebrate peace and cooperation, not violence.

In the 1993-1994 school year, I had many students who were difficult but also very intelligent. There were many personal issues they had to overcome, and showing them I cared was one of the main features of my teaching style. I spoke to B. N. about her behavior every other day in September and October, and by November and December I began to see some improvement. In January, the typical regression began to occur, and I talked to her in class for a minute--in between getting her to move her seat away from a boy with whom she was getting into verbal battles-- about going to lunch with me and a few others whom I had promised to take to McDonald's during the midyear break. Later, I discovered that she had told her mother and grandmother about the lunch invitation, which she had initially refused (mainly because it was soon after I had firmly disciplined her during classtime). She eventually did come to a pizza party that I held in school in February. Of course, she never told her mother or grandmother (who loved her and also cared enough to discipline her) about my need to discipline her.   I knew that my little "invitation" was worth more than all of the referrals to vice principals, phone calls to home, and moving her away from at-risk locations. It was the human approach, the protective factor; not the "you are the student (object) and I am the disciplinarian," that carried the real meaning for her.

Other factors--humor, reinforcement of students who may be at risk, self-discipline, and having one positive adult role model--are the best ways of building resilience and helping potentially at-risk youth or those youth who are already at risk from more failures inside and outside the school environment.

When the opportunities arose, B. N. was a speechmaker and a strongly opinionated writer. At times, I tried to encourage her to use those talents and allowed her to dramatize ideas when it was appropriate. In many ways, this began to build her self-esteem. As I continue to try to help her and others who act out in class, I realize that there are many informal and spontaneous ideas or methods that can succeed.

In as many cases as possible, I tried to find jobs for my students within my own middle-class neighborhood, a commercial area loaded with food franchises, small delicatessens, jewelry and clothing stores, small and large ethnic restaurants, and office buildings of all types. Within one year, I had placed four different tenth- through twelfth-grade students in after-school and weekend jobs in an informal way. Although there was a youth club which a history colleague had formally organized with businesses all over the city, my own small spontaneous efforts helped young people who chose to seek jobs by providing them with the assistance of a teacher whom they knew and trusted enough to go to directly as a resource. Without special tests but with a good word or two from me to a few managers, the young job hunters found that a decent application and one interview could quickly enable them to find a job and hold it for as long as they wished to do so. Many of these positions paid more than the minimum wage. I believe that teachers who work in schools with children who are poor are obligated not to give up on them, but to explain and give choices for the immediate issues in relationship to their lifelong alternatives.

Teachers need to validate whatever constructive choice a student makes--whether it be a vocational school curriculum, joining the armed services, or attending a good career school or a community college--before considering a regular public or private four-year college. If this means talking to parents or grandparents to validate young people's choices, so be it. Sometimes teachers are the only adults to do this for at-risk youth.

Recently, life and its strange twists and turns created an interesting encounter for me as a teacher. One Saturday in January 1994 at the Riverview Senior Citizen Center, a young twenty-three-year-old nurse's aide and I were discussing my eighty-three-year-old mother's extreme drowsiness. Ten days before that, my mother had returned from the hospital after being taken suddenly in an ambulance because she had not responded when a nurse tried to wake her for breakfast. It turned out, luckily enough, that my mother only had a minor infection. On that particular Saturday in January, my own profession came up in a conversation with the aide when a senior citizen resident asked me if I was working full time in Riverview. When I responded that I was a high school teacher at George Westinghouse High School, the aide acted startled and asked me if I knew her brother. Her brother, coincidentally, was the first student for whom I had found a job during the 1992-1993 school year. He had told her how I had searched and took him to the place of employment, after setting up the job ahead of time. The aide said that she could have used that kind of help in getting a job during her high school years. This incident drove home to me the fact that teachers do, at times, have a strong impact on poor youth who need jobs and social programs to help them and their families much more than they need incarceration or drug and/or alcohol rehabilitation in centers used as warehousing institutions. In simple language, our preventive work as individuals and as a society needs to catch up to our paradigm of the institutional punishment of criminals.

Jobs, social programs, trading in guns for money, and good school and recreational facilities, using dedicated teachers, counselors, clergy, and managers from the business community can generally create self-esteem, which can solve many of the problems leading to social trauma: drug addiction, poverty, serious crime, and weak communities. In the last month of 1993 and early in the 1994 school year, I saw the effects of my job-hunting assistance and the sensitive managers at certain franchises. I also saw shootings related to drug dealing and poverty in some inner-city neighborhoods. Those tragedies, of course, deeply affected students in the high school where I was teaching.

The Core Teams that do crisis intervention in all high schools need more personnel to work with the overwhelming numbers of troubled youth. Although some of my eleventh graders were finding jobs during the 1993-1994 school year, there was always the problem of poor attendance and other personal issues, which could hinder success at work. However, my first job find had enabled one eleventh grader to finish her eleventh month at a very good coffeehouse. By February 1994, she was considered a permanent staff member. By that same month, eight other students had asked me to help them find jobs, not counting D., the boy who had a job for seven months as a dishwasher. In a few cases, boys who were involved with the juvenile justice system began to inquire about my helping them find jobs (one mentioned that no one ever disciplined him at home when a teacher called to discuss his behavior). (This occurred one morning before the *Pittsburgh Post-Gazette's* reporting of youth talking to the Pittsburgh Human Rights Commission about their needs to help remove themselves from becoming at risk.) (Barnes 1994, C7).

In many cases, our youth have not demonstrated enough motivation to study regularly in school; nor can they always seek employment independently. How then can we expect them to build up enough confidence or self-esteem to graduate from high school, a vocational school, a community college, a university, or a career school? Are we training them well enough to do so? Can we motviate them? Can teachers help them achieve some economic independence? These are the major questions for teachers. If I could find five or six jobs for those high school students in one year, would their environment nonetheless cancel their chance to succeed? If they can claim one role model and get help in solving some personal and family problems as well, they may build up enough resilience to keep a part-time job. In a discussion with a colleague, I was told that teachers are making a difference. This person was optimistic that teachers do touch the students and help them to face the real world with a more positive attitude. She stated that she was an optimist. I suppose that most teachers are romantics and optimists. I assume that my school's present principal is one. So were Kozol, Neill, Froebel, Hemmings, Zutt, and others. So are all the dedicated counselors, teachers, social workers, principals, and sincerely interested business people who actively assist our at-risk youth to climb out of the abyss of despair. We all must try to help them do that. If they are doomed, so are we all.

Chapter 5

Opportunities for Change: The Real Chances to Provide Self-Esteem and to Prevent Warehousing of Our At-Risk Youth

Creating change for the large numbers of youth with low self-esteem who are either warehoused or killed before their twentieth birthday will require major efforts, including dismantling or remaking the ghetto communities of the North and the segregated South, at least in regard to attitudes if not institutions. Residential segregation is the institutional apparatus that supports other racially discriminatory processes; and both African-American and Hispanic economic minorities continue to suffer from America's effective system of subordination (Williams 1994).

In conversations with the best consultants of Eagle Ridge and the five-year federally funded A Chance for Youth Program, I have come to realize that the goal in Oklahoma City is to involve the entire community in the Oklahoma City poverty zones. It was understood from Day 1 that life skills programs, antidrug and alcohol discussions and videos, basketball leagues, cultural field trips, and training sessions for new volunteers would include children, parents, siblings in the various age groups, parishioners in the neighborhood, church leaders, and educators who lived or worked in the community.

The consulting psychologists have also begun to develop and implement youth support programs for the entire community as well as an outdoor six-month environmental peer group program, in which life skills and teamwork are taught every day in an encampment setting. As with the Youth Aliyah Rehabilitation Program in Kibbutz, the encampment programs are preceded by a preparatory workshop for three months called Operation GO (Great Opportunities for Youthful Offenders). This program is targeted at youth between the ages of ten and seventeen who are detained for crimes at the Oklahoma County Juvenile Detention Center. The program may be provided in the home, in the community, or at Eagle Ridge Institute.

In a few more years, Dr. Belinda Biscoe and the Eagle Ridge staff will begin to study the changes that the aforementioned programs enhanced in the Oklahoma City poverty zones. The eventual integration of youth from those neighborhoods into middle-class America will prove conclusively that such programs rehabilitate large numbers of youth in very disadvantaged communities; and our political decisions to pump money into them from the beginning will have saved lives and our society, in general, from hatred, fear, and crime that lead to serious urban degeneration and even collapse.

On May 10, 1994, I met for the first time Pittsburgh's Police Commissioner Gwen Elliot, who immediately understood the need for nonformal, long-range educational programs for at-risk youth in support-ive environments. By our second meeting in July, the commissioner had formulated a plan or concept that replicated the Youth Aliyah programs. At our initial meeting, this imaginative Commissioner, who had just be-come responsible for Youth Policy in the city of Pittsburgh, had requested an outline of such a Youth Aliyah Rehabilitation Program in Kibbutz. After reading a book or two and studying the outline, she realized the program's potential to rehabilitate our inner-city at-risk youth. In 1993 and 1994, the anticrime backlash in local and federal circles provided proof of the powerlessness of good social agencies, individual teachers, social workers, and psychologists since the 1980s. The fact that little funding reached major urban crime-ridden areas until the drive-by shoot-ings, armed robberies, murders, and overall recidivism began to outnum-ber successful rehabilitation on paper and in the public mind, proved that we were on the defensive.

There were numerous summits in 1993 and 1994. Gangs in Chicago, Kansas City, and Pittsburgh held summits and called truces, which were sustained to some degree or even very well at times. On the other hand, Chicago had thirteen shootings in a drug-related housing project in one week during the spring of 1994. A well known Chicago street counselor said that the truce would continue despite the shootings. However, few big cities have programs strong enough or of a duration to rehabilitate youth who shoot at each other and other victims in defense of their gang's territory or in competition for illegal business. There are also not enough well organized, comprehensive programs to prevent younger brothers and sisters from joining the criminal groups.

In an April 16 *Pittsburgh Post-Gazette* article (Barnes 1994), it was explained that the lack of legitimate identification items, such as driver's licenses, social security cards, and birth certificates, was hindering gang members from access to elemental services in our cities, the same services which the previous generations of immigrants and their children had used to advance their careers.

The mayor of Pittsburgh, Tom Murphy, continues to urge a $1 million budget from the state of Pennsylvania to aid in the establishment of a city/state partnership that "would provide alternatives for approximately 200 youth who will voluntarily leave the guns and participate in an intensive job preparation, placement, and training program" (Barnes 1994, C1, C7). One would hope that educational success would come to that group and that the funding would continue long enough for a preparatory socialization program to achieve positive results. As any understanding politician must realize, we must support at-risk youth with protective factors, since the family has not provided the nourishing such youth need. Such a group of youth could some day free itself from violence, shame, and despair. Such youth could then contribute in a positive way to their families, their neighborhoods, and city.

Mayor Tom Murphy believes he is providing a choice between the life of the gang, which will lead to incarceration or an early death, and entrance into economic and social stability through job training, mentoring, and counseling. This surge in Pittsburgh may have a local positive outcome and could provide a paradigm for other cities, such as New York, Chicago, and Detroit. We have known for almost a decade that job training and well organized social programs with capable staff, mentors, and efficient bureaucrats who do not scuttle the works, can succeed if enough time and patience are also available (Barnes 1994, C1, C7). If these factors are not available in abundance, anger and despair, lack of positive identification, and social and economic poverty will cause high-risk youth to use guns to purchase economic security and social status.

On the surface, good mediation programs in our schools that teach child care to teenage parents, as well as good outreach peer groupwork in the neighborhoods, can help stabilize a violent and hopeless community crime situation. However, cosmetic surface approaches are not capable of ending the behavior cycle of at-risk youth. Only the long-range and holistic approaches that rehabilitate and prevent acting out and the harmful behaviors we have seen in the last five to ten years can create meaningful outcomes for our society. Specifically, it will take many community-wide supportive recreational and social programs, good facilities, job training vocational programs, a coordinated group of men and women working together in a professional way, and strong family outreach programming within neighborhoods to dent the heavily weighted problems of our inner cities.

During my previous year at Westinghouse High School, I realized that the work process and teamwork were extremely important life skills for all of my eleventh-grade students to learn before graduating from high school. Many had characteristic at-risk teenage problems to deal with, including academic deficiencies and low self-esteem. Therefore, as the Archaeological Dig project (discussed next) developed between November 1993 and May 1994, I began to understand the social, economic, and psychological benefits the project had for the students. The actual digging for artifacts took place on May 4, 5, and 25; but the enthusiasm, high level of interest, and productive work and study on those days and on many others during the year were truly positive beyond the expectations of many. "The dig," as it was referred to, included building a sandbox, creating artifacts from clay, and then placing them by layers in the sand. As teams, students then dug for the artifacts, utilizing the archaeological process of drawing, recording, filming each artifact before answering our own research questions.

The eleventh-grade U.S. History archaeological dig was an amazing success, not because students were playing in the sand, but because many who were never eager to learn became involved to such an extent in this group project that they went far beyond themselves and remained on task for three and even four hours in unseasonably cold May weather, as well as throughout the training period before and after our spring break. In 1995, two new classes participated in a one-day dig. They were joined by a few veterans from the previous year; and after an evaluation, every teacher and student who participated agreed that it was an excellent experience that had become a tradition in our school.

D. X. was one girl who could be singled out, as was S. I., a boy who seldom arrived for class and who worked little when he did attend. Both of these youth were intelligent, possessed common sense, but could not usually relate very well academically. The teamwork that took place in the peer group setting helped the students who were academically weak to overcome their fears and enabled those who were initially responsible for photography to capture smiles and interest on the faces of their peers and friends working in and around the sandbox.

The idea of a two- or three-day peer group cooperative task is a good model for any long-range peer group cooperative program in a supportive environment. Although many inner-city youth try to learn within their capabilities, often they are overwhelmed by personal issues. Consequently, as youth who are isolated within their own cycle of failure and who have little home or community support, they thirst for and need the activities and guidance that will enhance positive attitudes and transcend despair, which submerges their self-discipline and ability to learn.

Peer group activities, such as the dig, will be the trend of the future since most American educators recognize the need to leave the standard textbooks and workbooks. Even in the better teaching universities, the written word is less important than group processes in problem solving. Since I recently taught high school students, using such techniques, I had become sensitive to backlash from a few of the traditional teachers who consider me more of an art teacher or a kindergarten-type displayer of the work of older children. However, at a recent Woodrow Wilson workshop for history teachers, many creative colleagues raised my hopes by saying that such an analysis of their teaching style would be taken as a compliment. Of course, hearing my students loudly proclaim, "I miss the dig!" or hearing them brag to their friends about how much fun they had working outside on the dig during those two or three days was enough empirical evidence for me to counteract the out-of-date and out-of-sync ideas of teachers who hang on to the controlling methods of the past. In *Death at an Early Age*, Jonathan Kozol relates an experience with an art teacher and a little sad boy named Stephen, who would give the art teacher little gifts of his drawings and comic strips while the art teacher screamed at the boy who, in the teacher's mind, could not do her formal art lessons correctly; that is, he wasted paper. Kozol understood the boy's need to be in his own creative world, since Stephen was small, ill, without parents, and often abused. His teacher only understood her need for control (Kozol 1990, 15).

Although most of our inner-city students watch violence and hear four-letter words on television and in most modern movies they see (except for an occasional *Sugar Hill*, which Claude Brown referred to as "an artistically eloquent and powerfully dramatic anti-drug film about a tragically drug-ravaged family struggling desperately to maintain its tenuous grip on life;" see Brown 1994, B3), there was not any confrontation or swearing at the hands-on activity of the dig. However, Claude Brown reasoned correctly when he wrote that movies and television shows that appeal to lower-class African-American youth, with their extreme violence and vulgar language, have created a new vernacular among our urban youth. He added that profanity has been making rapid progress in replacing the English language as the official language of the American people. In the same article, Brown summarized as follows: "We Americans have become a society of violence, addicts, and the media, which include the movie and music industries, are our drug dealers" (Brown 1994, B3).

The profanity syndrome analyzed by Claude Brown can be offset by the development of role models, who can educate our children to learn and enjoy social interaction without cursing. In some cases, we help our students find jobs, urge them to come to class, and try to help them overcome personal and family problems that overwhelm them. In other cases, we help our students enjoy learning by making learning fun (cheerleading before the dig, playing games, and other educationally positive activities that motivate at-risk youth). Teachers can help students by displaying humor about their own frailties as well as the students'.

We also have to learn how to express our caring and empathy to the youth whose despair, anger, and low self-esteem we see every day in our classrooms. In the school year of 1993/1994, I saw so much of those negatives that even if only a few freshman students said that their peers should show more respect to teachers, my short teaching career of eleven years in inner-city public schools would have been fulfilled. Since this did occur and since a small amount of other positive remarks were made, I felt that I had been rewarded. I also know that teachers who have been in those schools for twenty-five years or more feel that they have worked for the good of some students and have been positive role models for many over that period of time. The Neillian philosophy--giving love in abundance or else high-risk youth would absorb hate--came to fruition and those same students who needed to receive love were also able to return it. As I was giving a workshop in the summer of 1994, I realized that many inner-city teachers were dedicated and creative. One week later at a Woodrow Wilson History Seminar at Duquesne University, I realized this dedication and creativity by observing the activities demonstrated by many of the veteran teachers.

Under fire to produce good behavior and control, as well as relatively high standardized test scores and grades, many teachers have become cynical and have decided to learn survival skills, not teach them. However, there are many veteran teachers who are patient and caring. They create high-interest lessons and influence students' attitudes in positive ways. This will lead at-risk youth to acquire study and vocational skills and find decent jobs, which they will need for better careers in the next century. However, we are in need of other alternatives in the meantime--alternatives that will develop better attitudes and skills in order to survive, without crime, violence, drugs, and hate. Our major goal must be to raise the academic level and, through all the educational means available, create resilience for at least one out of every four youth in most of our cities and suburbs.

Alternative programs, such as the Youth Aliyah in Kibbutz Rehabilitation Program and A Chance for Youth, can be applied to my own city and many others as well. Gradually, in the last few years, *prevention* and *prosecution* have become the watchwords; but there are some youth who are already in the juvenile justice system and whose long-range alternative educational programs can change if we are wise enough to develop such programs soon.

Children who have been abused and have nowhere to turn will sometimes talk to teachers whom they trust. They may even write a request to talk to teachers in the hallway. The story is usually known before the student's appeal reaches the teachers. These teenagers are in need of the support of excellent counselors, psychologists, and teachers, as well as many other positive adults. The responsibility lies first and foremost with the professionals. We have to offer assistance if we expect such youth to remain in school. Eventually, only the alternative long-range programs will change the way the world will accept such students, but the students have to remain now in our own creative school programs.

Many of the students who have become alienated from society gradually become alienated from school, too. In their analysis of the High School and Beyond data, it was reported that there was a significant difference in attitudes regarding the academic aspects of school between sophomores who remained in school and those who dropped out of school. Of course, other reasons for school dropout include low self-esteem and increased school standards (Robenstein and Shultz, eds. 1994, 77, footnote 31). The other significant factors attributed to high dropout rates, according to the Office of Educational Research, are social class position, truancy, and high absenteeism (Robenstein and Shultz, eds. 1994, 77). All of the students who sought my help fit into those categories and were ready to drop out of school either by legal or illegal means. Of course, if they leave the system which we have established, they lose the educational benefits teachers try to provide; and then they lose the societal benefits, such as jobs, an opportunity to rise in the socioeconomic hierarchy, and a place in the future, void of poverty, failure, and crime.

Chapter 6

Conclusion: What Needs to Be Done

After reviewing the total picture of the alternatives to rehabilitate American at-risk youth, and after analyzing the recent articles and television debates about the preventative attempts by short-range programs outside of our cities (such as the relatively unsuccessful boot camps) and the inner-city after-school sports programs (such as Runs Batted In and Midnight Basketball [both of these programs have the aim to get at-risk youth off the street after school by organizing sports competitions, utilizing professionals when possible]), it has become clear that the long-range group programs in highly supportive environments and the community-based long-range social programs, such as A Chance for Youth, are the ones that most likely will prevent at-risk behavior and will save our children by supporting their resiliency and by rehabilitating them in the long run.

The Israeli Youth Aliyah programs, which were often based on the concept of *chevrat noar* peer group societies in the most idealistic communities, have already succeeded to such an extent that the most recent Israeli Army research of the 1980s depicts a much higher degree of motivation and higher scores overall (including intelligence, language, knowledge, logic, and attitude) in the original experimental group at Kibbutz Ramat Hakovesh than in the control groups, which served in the regular army without any previous program experience (Israeli Army Statistical Report, Tel Aviv Headquarters, 1985). The average score of the 46 or 47 was in comparison to the normal average of 42 of other groups.

Although the army rank of the experimental group was not necessarily higher, their total length of service in the Israeli fighting units was almost 15 percent higher than groups which had not previously been in other preparatory programs, including the Youth Aliyah ones. The higher motivation and the higher idealism scores in my previous research (Frank 1992) certainly would account for that 15 percent difference. In the *kibbutzim* of the left-wing Kibbutz Artzi movement, as in the early *Kvutzot*, the children's community had a wide measure of autonomy, just as in Neill's Summerhill. The intellectual influences of Freud and Marx and the philosophical support of Dewey and Piaget did come into play in such societies, but in the main, the youth were the ones who created their own extracurricular activities in each settlement (Near 1994, 242-247). As each one developed its own youth community, it set the pattern for leadership in the army of the State later, and pride and self-esteem were enhanced as more and more responsibility was taken in those communities after 1920. After their army service, the Youth Aliyah group, which has been in the Kibbutz Rehabilitation Program, was ready to go on with the careers of members' individual choices. Some were prepared to go to college, some to become army officers, some to learn a trade, and some to become kibbutz members.

The Oklahoma Boys Town Ranch also tries to use a similar framework to rehabilitate violent at-risk youth: work, studies, supportive adult models, and a positive relationship with a community inside a geographical area which is culturally similar to the school's values. In many instances, the Boys Town Ranch and the Cal Farley Ranch graduates at Amarillo, Texas could succeed to the same extent after graduation. Other cities could easily use these model programs and schools, as well as Alpha in the Detroit area (a highly successful alternative school in which students are involved in decisionmaking and credit allotment instead of being merely the recipients of grades for school work, work projects, etc.) to develop similar stories for hundreds of at-risk youth. In many communities and in many programs, education does take place within the context of the community. The community can be invited and welcomed into the school, and vice versa. The Boys Town Ranch and others have learned that this works. Other communities and the schools within them also are quickly learning this lesson.

Although Youth Aliyah no longer puts its major efforts into working with the inner-city youth of Tel Aviv, it hasn't ceased to change and adapt to the environment of Israeli needs. Therefore, special programs with newer Russian and Ethiopian immigrants have been succeeding in the *kibbutzim*, even though there are suddenly large numbers of adolescents who are at risk. One very experienced teacher and principal, Adam Ben Chanoch, who had been at Summerhill at the end of World War II and who had worked with at-risk youth in Israel for thirty-five years, told me in the summer of 1994 about some of the Russian youth whom he was counseling.

One story was filled with vivid details about R. She arrived in Israel from Russia with her divorced mother and stayed at kibbutz Kfar Giladi, one of the first *kibbutzim* with houses where children stay all day and all night, except for school and work time. R. was in the First Home in the Homeland program and was just fourteen when she arrived in the kibbutz. Adam described R. as short in stature, which made her look even younger than fourteen. "She had the figure of a budding young woman. She had the face of a pretty puppet, and the boys' looks followed her everywhere she went." Adam was then responsible for the special Hebrew program which most immigrant children take for some relatively short period of time upon arrival in Israel. When Adam met R., she had no knowledge of Hebrew. Adam said that at times her eyes gave the appearance that she was still in a dream or at least half asleep. There were many unhealthy stories about R.'s mother who had been seen searching in trash bins and loitering in an open market in Tel Aviv. The mother had been given a small flat away from the original one in Tel Aviv since she had been entertaining gentlemen for favors in the original Jewish Agency flat. Suddenly R. concluded her studies and Adam did not see her for a year.

A year later, Adam met R. as a part of the Youth Aliyah group of Russian immigrants studying at Har Ha Guy High School. His description of her follows: "She no longer appeared asleep or distant and, somewhat to my surprise, she had mastered the Hebrew language. R. seemed well motivated in her studies in class, with just a little problem in doing all her homework." I also learned from Adam that some of R.'s teachers had learned the trick of giving her a grade just above her achievement level to motivate her. When she did not receive high marks relative to other students, she became upset and even depressed, Adam reported. She was good in problem solving and in using her common sense, although her basic knowledge was not substantial. She usually did well in class discussions; but when she ran into opposition, she swore in Russian. (Her classmates told Adam that her fluency in swearing was astounding.)

R. gave the teachers a great deal of support in their attempt to create a positive learning environment in a class of immigrants, most of whom had failed in Russia and Israel. Her problems in the village of Gadot remained, however, since she had a boyfriend who brought her gifts and enticed her to stay out beyond the Youth Aliyah boarding school curfew. She could not understand why anyone could tell her not to smoke and when to turn off her lights at night. One day, Adam was ready to return one of her fantasy stories, which consisted usually of her dreams in both Russia and Israel, when he discovered that she was not in class. Other students told him that R.'s mother had just driven into Gadot with a well-dressed gentleman and taken R. out of the program. Adam later learned that R.'s mother insisted that she needed R. at home for financial support. R. would work as a photographer, a model, and acquire a good trade. Despite all sorts of trepidation, Adam said that he felt that R. was strong willed and resilient enough to stand on her own two feet, since Youth Aliyah had worked with her for more than a year. Indeed, she would stand on her own two feet.

It is apparent from this story and many others in Israel and the United States that immigrant children can be integrated and become resilient if the walls of traditional schools are broken down and the leadership of alternative programs understand the cultural backgrounds that students bring to school as well as the nonformal methods of such successful programs. As the social issues of youth changed in Israel and as the cultural backgrounds of the at-risk youth became more diverse during the 1970s and 1980s into the 1990s, Youth Aliyah continued to adapt. This is what Eagle Ridge was attempting to do in the poverty zones of Oklahoma City, moving beyond walls of schools into the communities. There, all the inhabitants are involved: the families of the children, artists and musicians, day care workers, the retired and unemployed adults who watch children as they walk home from school, the volunteers from the churches, and even ex-prisoners who want to help others. Many of the children were (and still are) from newer immigrant groups, and may of the staff of A Chance for Youth are as well.

The students whom I have encountered during the last three years of my teaching career have encouraged me by their personal resilience, as well as by the way they have related to me, to research the topic of resilience in the modern educational and psychological literature. For high-risk youth, this variable may be a saving device from the pain and suffering created by dysfunctional family lives or the environment. I believe this occurs to an extent beyond the comprehension of the most dedicated teachers, social workers, and psychologists.

In their book *The Resilient Self*, Steven J. Wolin and Sybil Wolin have named seven major characteristics that make up the Challenge Model for "sufferers." This model includes seven factors that lead to resiliency and can help our at-risk youth overcome the major problems that victimize them as well as constantly lower their self-esteem (Wolin and Wolin 1993, 21). I have been observing ten or more students at George Westinghouse High School using these traits, and it is uplifting to realize that probably hundreds of more young people are doing so in my city of Pittsburgh as well as in many other areas of the United States. The seven factors in the Challenge Model are independence, insight, humor, creativity, relationships, morality, and initiative (Wolin and Wolin 1993, 21). All of these factors are of equal importance and do not appear in any particular order in the book by Wolin and Wolin. In fact, the Wolins refer to the Mandala, which is similar to a Jungian archetype as a circular figure projecting the self (the latter never has been analyzed in a particular order).

In one chapter of their timely and insightful book, the Wolins use their Challenge Model to overcome the Damage Model. Their model uses reframing to include resilience as well as parental faults, thereby giving the power to change (Wolin and Wolin 1993, 5, 21, 59-60). Many of my students lacked self-esteem because of their family situations. According to the Wolins,

When parents behave as if they, themselves, are their one and only child; when parents do not provide a stable, safe, and supportive environment; when parents abuse, neglect, coerce, and criticize; when parents do not serve as role models or offer guidance; when parents and children mismatch, then children can't be children. Instead they become ugly, bad, and unacceptable in their own eyes. (Wolin and Wolin 1993, 47)

Therefore, the key is to experiment with creative activities and branch out in support of and guidance to young people; and for young people to act on their own behalf if they are to use resilience to limit the damage that parents and the environment can cause. The personal traits and the protective factors caring adults use do not specifically use the Challenge Model, but the psychologists who have written and used them in their work (e.g., Werner and Biscoe) relate directly in theory and practice to those very resiliencies about which the Wolins have written. All of the models in one way or another attempt to shift the balance between stress and protection, vulnerability and resilience.

B. L. was a wonderful person for me to follow in the House since even after he had studied with me during the first semester that I was there, he somehow managed to appear in my second year at lunch time or before homeroom time. During that free time, he either helped me write a few questions on the board, asked me to lend him a dollar, or talked about his basketball skills and his grades (especially if he was in danger of failing one subject), or we discussed all of those topics in one short five- or ten-minute time span. One morning, he even told me about a fight he was almost involved in between two gangs. I learned to see his humor and bravado as his well-organized defense mechanisms, and I knew that he had higher levels of academic skills than most of his peers. I also began to understand how hard he had to work to say away from peer issues that would create big problems for him, and I saw that he had succeeded by the end of his junior year. I also understood how much a strong male role model could mean to him. In his senior year, B. L. was maturing and by November 1994, our discussions shifted to colleges and the relevancy of high grades and a high-quality educational experience. He finally began to attend every class and was eligible to play on the basketball team for the first time. One day, B. L. began to push me to come to the first game and show school spirit, which I interpreted as, "Come and see me play." By that time, I realized that his resiliency had developed partly because of me; and because his own inner strength (independence) and humor fit so well with his intelligence.

V. was another student of mine during the first year at George West-inghouse High School. My first effort to build her self-esteem with a Student of the Month Award led her to see me as a friend. She had been a good student earlier when she had been in a special Advanced Placement class; but because of her poor attitude towards academics and her being somewhat spoiled at home (a fact that her mother admitted to me), V.'s grades were tapering off by her junior year. Although I tried many methods to motivate her in my United States History class, I did not succeed until one day I learned that she had an African-American role model who was a writer and that she really wanted to be a writer herself. In her senior year, V. and I were still good friends; and she came to my classroom every day to visit me. One day, there was a bulletin announcement that a poem that she had written had been published in an African-American magazine. When I told her that I had heard the announcement, which she had missed, her eyes lit up and she asked me to post the announcement on the bulletin board, which I did that day. From then on, I received sometimes two visits a day; and we began to discuss how she should continue to develop her writing skills, plan for college, and read more than she had been reading during her early high school years. Although V. was not attending any of my classes that year, our friendship became stronger, and by September of 1995, there were signs that she was preparing to attend a good college. Even her dress style changed from those "wanna-be" clothes of her sophomore year to a young collegiate style. Later, she wrote an article against gang life, which had hurt or killed many of her peers. The article appeared in a city school paper. I saved the article and told V. that I would like to use it for my book. At first she did not believe me, so I had to repeat what I had said. The following is a quote from her article: "This is a lesson for all gang members. Listen to others who give helpful advice on ways to get out of gangs--the easy way before it's too late."

In the school year 1993-1994, I taught one ninth-grade class of Science and Math (S.A.M.) students, who were extremely noisy in class and very immature in their attitudes toward school work and others. The chemistry between many of the boys and girls was not right, and some of the girls were too social because of their history together in middle school. Although I had worked hard to give them support, I never felt that I was able to raise their level of maturity during that year. However, during the 1994-1995 school year, I did see many of them in the halls near my classroom; and I remained on a friendly basis with a good number of them, often saying as we passed each other, "Hi, what's new?" Of that group of twenty-five, I felt that two of the girls (W. C. and B. C.) were particularly resilient and generally creative and were on the right path toward independence.   Both of these girls demonstrated a strong motivation to succeed academically (unlike the previous year, during which their absenteeism was flagrant). W. C. and B. C. held my interest, and a third person, R. N., did so even more. Although I felt that W. C. and B. C. had good chances to succeed without having the chances other children had, R. N. had an even better chance to have a good career, despite the fact that she often acted out and was stubborn.

Although the first two teenage girls had mothers who attempted to guide them, both girls were absent from school so often during the first semester, because of circumstances beyond their control at times, that it was difficult to work with them and stabilize their learning patterns and their overall behavior in class. Both related well to me, more as a father figure or an older role model, since I encouraged them to learn and was usually kind to them. I brought them treats when they did well each week or two (often these treats were books, not just the typical candy bar). They became close to me by the end of the school year, and one of them even said that she would fight anyone who antagonized me in class. When I saw them the following year, I noticed that their moods were positive; that they were doing well in their classes; and that their attendance had greatly improved. My overall impression was that they were handling problems in a more mature way--problems that had overcome them the previous year.

The third girl, R. N., was a student with two parents at home, both of whom had full-time jobs. R. N. was intelligent, sensitive, vocal, and argumentative. She talked often to girlfriends in her class, and in particular to one boy, who was also bright but also in trouble inside and outside school. R. N. had difficulty relating in a polite way to many of her teachers during her first year, and I saw that she was not given some privileges that other S.A.M. students received after the first semester. However, by October 1994, I saw her and spoke with her in the hallway three or four times and learned that she was arguing fairly often with only one teacher. R. N. was finally acting as if she knew more about self-discipline and reaching her academic potential, which I felt was very high. During the 1993-1994 school year, my ability to get her to work hard on self-discipline was not significant. However, in discussing that and other related issues during the 1994-1995 school year, I felt progress had been made and I wanted it to continue. My main goal was to convince R. N. that in the long run it would be beneficial for her to discipline herself and accept teacher criticisms when necessary. Since we had a decent relationship and I tried to treat her as a bright young lady, she accepted most of my points. Although it is too early to tell, I believe she has the potential creativity, intelligence, and sensitivity to adjust successfully to high school and to someday attain a fine professional career in the humanities. In the meantime, I felt that I could speak to her in the halls and watch her progress.

I am now certain that the support I gave to the three girls during 1993-1994 was showing signs of progress. I had been moving into the position of being an adult role model, and they could now (November 1994) relate to me on an informal basis. Because of V., B. L., and R. N., and other young people whom I have recounted in this chapter, I have learned that teachers can help create and reinforce resiliency among many high-risk youth.

In October of 1994, I met L. B. and realized after three or four weeks in class that he and a friend in the same class were two resilient young men who had experiences and opinions about group homes, juvenile detention centers, and the infamous Wagon Train. These two young men had hoped to survive without repeat performances in any of those institutions. L. B. said that he had learned not to use muscle when someone tried to put him down or degrade his attempts to succeed based on feelings of superiority. Instead, he would try to use his brains.

L. B. was especially articulate, and so was his friend, O., I would later learn. In my World Cultures class, we spoke about politics, history, sociology, religion, and many other relevant topics in mostly a spontaneous fashion. All of the boys who attended the class liked discussing the issues of the day and their feelings about those issues, without rejecting the classwork that I assigned that day. Somehow, we finished all of the classwork with ease, and there were seldom discipline problems. Since two of the students had traveled a great deal and a few others were also somewhat articulate, it was easy to touch on many of the problems of at-risk youth and, at the same time, relate directly to current politics (e.g., the results of the November 1994 elections and their impact on minority youth). L. B. and O. also had a number of discussions with me on how to rehabilitate high-risk youth, and they told me that they spoke often to younger children in their neighborhoods and tried to influence them to stay out of trouble. They also said that they thought they could be good counselors in a peer group program.

By November of that school year, I began to sense that the two of them had a chance to succeed if they would continue to have such positive attitudes and if they would stay out of trouble with the police. Although I knew that L. B. had read a good deal, I was still in awe of his knowledge and his articulate expression. One example of this occurred one day in the library, when he explained to the school librarian and me the detailed history of the Nat Turner revolt. After that experience, I understood that in some way I needed to help L. B. finish high school and apply himself in a formal higher educational system, from which he could develop into a professional who could some day help other young people. Based on my observations of him, I also decided that he was already overcoming his difficulties by using intelligence, independence, and common sense to give himself a chance for a successful future. Since he stated a number of times how he liked my history class, I reached the conclusion that I had a chance to help him reach his goals. In my mind, his resilience was already well developed, and he could trust one adult to assist him in succeeding because of that resilience.

Late in November, the principal told me that he would like to meet L. B. In a short discussion, the principal told L. B. that he had the reputation of not being a positive leader in the middle school nearby. (In fact, his status had been above the principal's and certainly well above the vice principal's there.) L. B. said that he had changed a lot since then and that he definitely was no longer a gang member. Whether being on the Wagon Train program or just time to be away and think had helped is not well documented, but certainly his independence and native intelligence had been factors. At this writing, I hope to be able to see him soon develop into a good peer group leader in some program. I am somewhat optimistic about his surviving and, in a few years, studying in a formal setting far from the environment in which he is still struggling.

My last story is a rather long one which was related to me as an assignment by a bright Education major at Duquesne University. I believe that to get the full impact of this account of a resilient young person who knew how to seek out a caring teacher to be his role model, it is best to quote the story in its entirety. The Education major began the story by writing that she was a tutor in an after-school tutorial program located in the inner-city projects:

Before leaving today, I worked with Richard on his phonics. This is my second time working with Richard. He is a really cute kid, and you can see his great personality under the front he puts up. He has no motivation whatsoever. He did not want to do his homework, and I practically begged him to get started. I tried praising him every time he got the right answer, and I modeled the correct response. He wanted me to give him the answers. I refused, and he got angry. *(It is typical of at-risk kids to get angry in that case.)*

I entered the building today to find it in its usual chaos [my italics]. I went upstairs looking for Richard. He was up there, and he had phonics homework. He did not want to do his work, and something was going on with some of the other kids. I kept encouraging him because I knew something was going on, and I did not want to yell at him.   All of a sudden Antwon came into the room, and Richard stood up, and they started yelling. *Richard went over to Antwon and got in his face; I stood in between. Richard was pushing into me, and Antwon was pushing into me; I somehow talked them out of punching each other's heads in. I told Antwon to go into another room. Richard would not tell me what they were fighting for, and he said it was "none of my business." I let it drop and tried to get him back to work* [my italics]. Other kids kept coming in trying to cause trouble. I could see that it was going to be a miracle if anything was to be accomplished that day. Richard sat there grumpily and would not listen to anything I said. He said that he hated school, and he didn't care. Another tutor and I tried to talk to him. We asked him what he wanted to be when he grew up; he said a basketball player. I told him that he had to go to college, so he better start caring about his schoolwork. He said he would start his own team. He did not want to do any work and another child came in and asked me for help. I said I would help him, and Richard got angry and said, "You're supposed to be helping just me." I told him that I could help both of them. He slammed his book shut and said, "Forget you," and walked out. He came back and started talking to me later. He told me that he only cares about his friends and his family. He told me why he and Antwon were fighting. I asked him if he would try and be in a good mood when I came back on Wednesday. He said, "I don't make promises." I told him to try.

I decided to take my camera today to take pictures for my portfolio. I walked upstairs and peeked in one of the rooms, not knowing what mood Richard would be in. He said, "Come here." He took my hand, led me into the room and said, "You're the only one who can help me with my homework." I couldn't believe it! My investment finally paid off. I tried to hide my astonishment, and I took his hand and we walked into the room. He sat down and started to work. It took some encouraging to get him to work, but he definitely was in a better mood. *Antwon came in, and they began to scuffle again. I broke them up and tried to stop the name calling. I have no idea what they were fighting about today. He started his work again; he noticed my camera. I told him that if he did all his work, he would be able to take pictures with my camera* [my italics]. After he finished, we got out the camera. Each of the kids took turns taking a picture. I kept wondering if they were cutting off everybody's head. They were excited to use the camera, and I told them that I was trusting them with it. I told Richard that I wanted a picture of him and Antwon together, but he refused. Toward the end I was able to get them in the picture together.

When I entered the room today, Richard called me by name and asked for help. I sat down and decided to go with the flow. I reached into my purse for something, and he noticed my wallet. He asked if he could look at my pictures. I gave him my wallet and told him who everybody was. We looked at the pictures for a while. He then asked me for a dollar. I told him that I didn't have a dollar. He asked for a quarter, and I told him that I couldn't give him a quarter. There were three other boys in the room, and they all started. I said that I didn't have any; they didn't believe me. I looked and saw that I only had three quarters and there were four of them. I tried to put them back in my wallet when Richard grabbed my hand and said, "Please." I tried to take the quarters out of his hand; he gave one to Antwon (Surprise, they must be friends today.). Kevin, one of the smaller boys, got mad and kicked Antwon, which started a fight. Kevin was really angry. I tried to break them up; Richard held Antwon back and told him to settle down I was really shocked; usually he is the one fighting. *I felt terrible and was out of control. I was mad at myself for even getting in the situation. I honestly did not know how to handle it* [my italics].

I was surprised that a quarter would set them off like that. As I thought about it, I realized that they probably see their family fight over money all the time. Something as small as a quarter to me obviously was bigger to them. *The episode definitely taught me that I'm not able to handle every situation handed to me* [my italics].

I looked for Richard when I came in today; he was at the computers. It was a nice day, so there were not a lot of children to tutor. I waited to help someone. Finally, group two came back from the computers. Richard, Antwon, and Dereck said they had homework. We went upstairs, and they said they just wanted to avoid "Miss Cranky's" math class. I told them that they had to do work if they wanted to stay up here with me. They agreed; we ended up doing a lot of talking while working. They told me that it was Dereck's birthday, and I should give them money. I was not going to mess this up again; I stood firm and told them that I didn't have any money. They dropped it, and I continued working on phonics with Richard. I tried to get him to think a little more for himself. I told him that I would be there if he had a question, but I wanted him to try and figure out the answer for himself. I wanted to try and use Vygotsky's zone of proximal development. He didn't like the idea; he needed me there as security. Richard doesn't feel that he knows the answer, and he needs someone to tell him that he is correct. He is tough on the outside, but it is because he is insecure.

He said that he had an important question for me. I braced myself, and he said, "How come you can see lipstick so much better on white girls? When my mom wears lipstick, you can hardly tell she has any on!" I tried not to laugh, but it was funny. I told him that I had to leave soon, so we better finish his phonics. He responded to that by saying, "Can I come with you?" At that moment, everything that we had been doing up until that moment didn't matter. *After all the time I had invested in him, he let me know, in his own way, that he cared. I wanted so much to tell him that I would take him home with me. It broke my heart to tell him that he had to stay there* [my italics].

Recently I have learned about another good peer group, community-based program in Pittsburgh, one with a branch right inside my school. It is called the Family Support Center. Although it began to recruit teenage parents only six months ago, its goals, the dedication of its staff, and its positioning in the community from which our school draws its students lead me to believe that it will succeed.

Although there are few statistics that prove how social changes occur in at-risk youth, this chapter has been an attempt to demonstrate explicitly that well-organized, long-range programs in supportive environments or inside disadvantaged communities by excellent psychologists, counselors, and teachers, as well as individual efforts by teachers in schools, can build on the resiliency of large numbers of at-risk youth. The outcomes from this type of effort will be much better than little or no effort. Love and caring are the base of these efforts, and financial support by our society is the next ingredient. Once those two elements exist, Youth Aliyah or Boys Town Ranch programs or A Chance for Youth or Family Support centers could be activated. All of these paradigms have been explained and well illustrated in this book and in brochures, and even in some cases have been supported by reliable statistics. The risk in any case is better than the do-nothing attitude of some politicians and bureaucrats in our society. More teachers who care must also be trained, and this will have to occur in a short time period since violence and its roots are tearing at the heart of our society at a rapid rate. Punishment will not solve our problems with a growing number of our youth--despair and desperation will overcome our youth. Instead, there is a need to develop programs that can prevent and rehabilitate youth who are already at risk, building on their resiliency and a caring and professional expertise. Soon, it will be too late. Riots and urban warfare could be the result. The 1860s and 1960s have served notice to society. It is time to awaken to a new call; it is time to work toward the solutions of the major issues, which is how to build self-esteem in our at-risk youth.

In writing this summary, I had to remind myself that the purpose of putting together this book is to present to the scholarly reading audience and to the intelligent parent and professional youth worker the difficulties our children have in becoming adults, as well as to present the programs and types of professionals who can assist in the rehabilitation and prevention of at-risk behaviors. In the 1990s, at-risk youth include not only teenagers but younger children in middle schools and elementary school children as well. I met many of the former in Pittsburgh and Oklahoma, as well as in Israel in the 1970s and 1980s. I met many younger children in programs in the late 1980s and in the 1990s. I also worked with hundreds of at-risk youth in the Three Rivers Youth programs in the 1980s and in George Westinghouse High School in the 1990s. In many cases I have seen resiliency, and in many cases I have seen excellent peer group programs. I have also seen my own at-risk daughter grow up and become independent and successful in college beyond the expectations of some social workers and psychologists. Finally, she has grown into a sensitive and caring person.

In my overall analysis, I have found many successful attempts to build self-esteem in children through some programs in the United States; but there have also been delays that have led to the loss of good children. Decent programs were not receiving necessary support, and many researchers and local bureaucrats were stonewalling the fulfillment of progressive ideas that could have made a difference. The potential to or-ganize and act is still alive in teachers, counselors, psychologists, and so-cial workers; but many battles have been lost. In some instances, a major revolt or civil war is a possibility which (as shown by the revolts in New York in 1861, and Cleveland and Los Angeles in the 1960 riots) could create much damage to the infrastructure and the soul of our urban life. It is still early enough to act in the environment of those urban areas, both large and small, as well as in the supportive environments that accommo-date long-range peer group programs. These programs will have to in-clude excellent staffs of counselors and teachers as well as positive role models. The entire community in which such programs exist must also be active in attempts at prevention and rehabilitation. The cost will be much less than the warehousing and violence that at-risk youth can create. Only with the use of the models presented in this book can a viable society be rebuilt in which all can live peacefully, knowing that the utmost has been done for the American youth of the 1990s.

Epilogue

In the two to three weeks since I finished writing this book, one book review in the *New York Times*, at least two additional articles, and one NBC
1994 news report claimed that teenage violence during the period from
1985 - 1994 has increased at the rate of double the shooting deaths; and
50 percent more African American victims in the fifteen- to twenty-four-
year-old range. One of the two articles depicted how difficult it was to
survive in the ghetto in Philadelphia: "Nationally, crime is down. In poor
black urban areas, it's increasingly hard to avoid. Just ask Boo Sampson."
The article, which appeared in the Sunday *Philadelphia Inquirer*, went on
for three pages, describing the misery and despair of urban ghetto youth.
"On my block, all people talk about is getting high" (Zuchinno 1994, A1,
A22, A23).

   Those articles and the news report only verified and reinforced what I
already knew was occurring in middle-sized cities, such as Chester,
Pennsylvania, not just in Philadelphia, Chicago, and New York. What
most caught my eye appeared in the December edition of the *Jewish
Chronicle* of Pittsburgh. It was an article about the United States
Secretary of Health and Human Services visiting one of those Youth
Aliyah unique educational long-range program facilities. This one, at
Yemin Orde, was called a Youth Village and worked with immigrants
from Ethiopia and Russia, and troubled urban Israeli youth. To quote
Donna Shalala's impression, "The model is very famous. The village is a
stop for everyone in the United States interested in children, education,
and the family" (Mann 1994, 37). What she did not say was that Youth
Aliyah not only changed to meet the needs of immigrant youth but was
still rehabilitating its own high-risk children simultaneously. What was
more meaningful, however, was the viewpoint of Shalala's counselor.
Peter Edelman said that it was a wonderful program but not easily replicated since you cannot use such residential programs on a large scale in
America to solve the problems of our youth. Edelman expressed his
doubts because we lacked resources and expertise. In fact, the United
States can and must find the resources; the United States definitely has

the expertise or has its own models from which it can learn. Training is not the problem. America must have the will to develop such programs. There are no alternatives. In the same article, it was mentioned that a private foundation was planning to build such a Youth Aliyah village in the Philadelphia area and that the Detroit municipality was also planning to use the model, despite the federal government's negative reaction. I believe that such organizations can build their own successful programs. My hope is that their model will become part of the American landscape in the near future.

Although the long-range peer group which I recommend in *Children in Chaos* and in this book as well is usually more successful than incarceration or even more short-term recreational programs after school (with an occasional drug and alcohol counseling program added), it has become clear that advocacy and other one-on-one relationships, which include counseling for families, have also become part of a new wave of American programming to rehabilitate at-risk youth. Teachers, social workers, and youth counselors are involved in this mode of action. A recent *New York Times* series described such a program at the cost of $4,000 a year for each offender or potential juvenile delinquent. This program can save children from crime, violence, and prison (which cost the public $40,000 to $60,000 a year at some late date in the youth's life). The relationships that are detailed in the December 1994 articles (Wilkerson 1994, A1 and A10, and Treaster 1994) prove how individual caring and professional organizations can help make a difference in the lives of children. Because one particular program's counselors have a maximum of thirty cases and they frequently visit, intervene, and counsel youth, the program apparently has created deep enough relationships (counselors are basically acting as surrogate parents) to make a positive impact on the life of each at-risk youth. These recently initiated programs convinced me that my own relationships with students could create "the margin of victory." My discussions revolve around youth staying out of trouble, as well as my helping them in the classroom and with job searches. My goal is to enable them to become positive about themselves and become constructive citizens in a society that is in need of such young people.

At this time in America's social and political history when regressive attitudes are holding sway in Congress (e.g., the statement that orphanages and more secure warehousing for our children will save money and cut down on crime or at least wreak vengeance on those who assault others), youth are in need of more moral and social support than ever before. Their families, and at times even their entire communities, need as much real educational assistance as can be afforded so we can enable them to create a belief in their own abilities and a chance to work hard and rise up from the poverty and disintegration of their lives. This demands new atti- tudes and a renewed sense of power, which individual professionals can promote in an organized manner. *Headstart* is a perfect example. Such achievements as *Headstart* will not occur if we use the "mean methods" of Gingrich and Company. Such a reactionary and antieducational style is not becoming of this nation, nor will it solve our deepening problems, which are both human and spiritual in nature just as much as they are economic and political.

Appendix I

Contents for Curriculum: Leadership Training and Drug and Alcohol Prevention and Intervention (1988)

Appendix II

Session V: Peer Pressure

Activity

Get the Picture?

<u>Purpose</u>:   To help teens become aware of themselves, their likes and dislikes, unique qualities and future goals

<u>Materials</u>:   Newsprint sheets and markers for each group member; scissors and glue; discarded magazines, newspapers, catalogues, etc., for clipping

<u>Time</u>:   40 - 50 minutes

<u>Procedure</u>:   1, 2, 3

Give each teen a piece of newsprint and a marker. Instruct teens to fold their newsprint sheets in half and write at the top of each half, "This is me!" and "This is my future!" (as illustrated below):

Now tell them to cut pictures, words, drawings, and phrases from the magazines that symbolize things about themselves and their futures. For the side labeled, "This is me!" examples might include physical traits and parts of the body, clothes, hobbies, or achievements, personality traits, etc. These should all be glued into place to form a collage. For the other side labeled, "This is my future!" suggestions might include travel, personal possessions (e.g., cars or houses), children, careers, vacations, money, or any aspect of future life. These can be glued into place on the remaining side of the newsprint sheet.

DISCUSSION

<u>Points</u>:

1. Did anyone use positive and negative symbols for "me?" All positive? All negative? Why?

2. Is it difficult or easy to imagine what the future will be like?

3. Did anyone put the same or similar symbol on both sides to symbolize that "what is *me* today will be *me* in the future?"

Activity

Interview about Me

Purpose: To give teens the opportunity to learn what positive qualities others see in them

Materials: Activity Worksheet, "Interview about Me"

Time: Two or three days for individuals; 30 minutes for group discussion

Procedure: 1, 2, 3

Introduce this activity by telling your group that sometimes other people recognize our strengths even better than we do. Hand out the Interview Form and instruct teens to write their names in the center and then complete the box labeled, "Myself" by writing in it those things which they like about themselves. Then tell them their task is to choose four other boxes on the form and interview the person described in it. During the interview, they are to ask the question, "What are three things you like about me?" and record those answers in the appropriate box. Be sure you name a date and time by which the interview must be completed and arrange for a time to discuss this activity at your next meeting, using the following discussion points.

DISCUSSION

Points:

1. How does it feel to learn what people like about you?

2. Were you surprised to learn about some strengths you didn't know you had?
3. Were you disappointed if no one mentioned a strength you consider important? How can you make people more aware of that strength?
4. Did more than one person name the same positive quality about you?
5. Do you remember to tell people around you what you like about them?

Activity Worksheet

Interview about Me

Under the heading, "Myself," list three things *you* like about yourself. Then interview four of the remaining people and ask them to name any three things *they* like about you as a person. Write their answers under the appropriate heading.

MYSELF   **PARENT OR GUARDIAN**

BROTHER OR SISTER   **AN ADULT**

A TEACHER   **A NEIGHBOR**

A MALE FRIEND   **A FEMALE FRIEND**

Appendix III

Session XVI: Drug and Alcohol Information

Compelling Future in 3-D:
A Leadership Training and Drug and Alcohol Prevention and Intervention Curriculum, 1988

ACTIVITY: "Facts or Fiction"
Game Show

TIME: 60 Minutes

MATERIALS: Game Show Questions
Bells or Buzzers
Velcro Stickers
Construction Paper

VOCABULARY:

OBJECTIVES:

1. To help participants differentiate facts from myths related to chemical use, abuse, and dependency
2. To help participants assess the impact of chemical abuse and dependency on the individual, family, society
3. To provide information on prevention strategies

PROCEDURE

Create a game show board which simulates the diagram at the end of this activity. The game board has seven categories across. In each category there are ten questions with increasing value based on the question's difficulty as you move down the board. Draw round circles on construction paper in a variety of colors. Label each circle with the appropriate point value. On the back of each circle, glue a Velcro^{TM} backing, which is attached to a Velcro base, which is glued on the poster board. This allows a question to be easily lifted off the board. The questions should by typed on small pieces of paper and glued or taped to the back of the circle. Below the question should be the answer.

GAME RULES

Divide participants into two teams. Flip a coin to decide which team goes first. Team members should line up on opposite sides of the room and face the game board and the facilitator who is the game show host.

Make sure each team has a bell or buzzer to signal that they want to answer. Each team's signal should have a different sound. The first member of each team should be handed the buzzer/bell. The team which won the flip of the coin is the first to select a category and value. The facilitator pulls the question from the board and directs it to the first two team members. The first team member to signal is given an opportunity to respond to the question. If their response is incorrect, the participant on the opposite team is given a chance to respond. If it is a true/false item, the other team is not allowed to respond. If neither team knows the answer, both teams have ten seconds to huddle to come up with the correct response. The first team to signal gives their response. If their response is correct, they receive the appropriate points. Their second team member then selects the next category and point value. If the team gives an incorrect response, the other team is given the opportunity to answer and the same process follows. If neither team gives the correct response, the facilitator gives the answer but points out that discussion will follow later. When neither team gives a correct response, a coin should be flipped again to determine who starts the new round.

The facilitator should serve as game show host or hostess and keep the score for each team.

Point out to the participants at the end of the game that this was not intended to be a win/lose situation; instead, this was a fun way to begin separating facts from fiction related to chemical use and abuse.

After the game show, the facilitator should tell participants that they will discuss these issues in more depth at the next session. It is important in this session to complete the game. Session XVI will provide an opportunity for discussion. The information on the questions in this session can serve as the basis of discussion in the next session.

ADDITIONAL DIRECTIONS ON GAME BOARD
CONSTRUCTION

Glue two pieces of poster board together so that the length of your game board is approximately 3 feet 7 inches by 2 feet 4 inches. If the poster board is thin, additional pieces can be glued to the back for support. A stand can be made to support the board or two holes punched at the top with a cord tied through them so that the board can hang. However, standing it against something will work just as well.

The circles should be no more than 3 inches in diameter. By using different colors of construction paper, the board is visually appealing to students. The title, "Facts or Fiction" can be cut in block letters and glued on the board. Finally, Velcro circles can be placed on the back of the circles and the board for easy placement and removal.

FACTS OR FICTION?

High on the Hit Parade	Chemicals and You	Drugs Ok?	The Drug Boutique	Ounce of Prevention	Never-Never Land	Designer "Genes"
10	10	10	10	10	10	10
20	20	20	20	20	20	20
30	30	30	30	30	30	30
40	40	40	40	40	40	40
50	50	50	50	50	50	50
60	60	60	60	60	60	60
70	70	70	70	70	70	70
80	80	80	80	80	80	80
90	90	90	90	90	90	90
100	100	100	100	100	100	100

HIGH ON THE HIT PARADE

POINT VALUE	QUESTION	ANSWER
10	Most cocaine addicts also become addicted to heroin or alcohol.	True

In general, people who are addicted to one drug are also at risk for addiction to other chemicals. The biochemical imbalance that many individuals seem to have makes them more susceptible to becoming addicted to any kind of chemical. The research of a medical scientist in Houston supports this finding. The Houston Police Department made available the bodies of skid row bums for her to use in her cancer research. While doing studies on their brains, she discovered a substance in chronic alcoholics that is closely related to heroin. This substance is called telrahychoisoquinoline, or THIQ for short. In normal social drinking, alcohol is rapidly eliminated--about one drink per hour. Alcohol is first converted into a chemical called acetaldehyde. If too much of this builds up in our system, we become very ill. Our bodies eliminate acetaldehyde by changing it into acetic acid, or vinegar, and then finally into carbon dioxide and water, which is then eliminated in our kidneys and lungs.

Researchers in Houston discovered that in alcoholics, very small amounts of acetaldehyde are not eliminated; instead, it goes to the brain where it is stored as THIQ. THIQ has been found to be very addictive. No research has determined how much THIQ must build up before a person becomes alcoholic. In predisposed persons, it can happen very early in their youth. Once it occurs, the alcoholic will be as addicted to alcohol as he would have been to heroin had he/she been using that drug. Alcoholism is a disease, but with proper treatment, the drinking can stop. While alcoholics can't rid themselves of THIQ, they can be taught to live healthy lives without the use of chemicals.

POINT VALUE	QUESTION	ANSWER
20	What drug causes the heart to beat 50 percent faster?	Cocaine

Irregular heart action related to cocaine use occurs, and cases of myocardial infraction have been reported in men, aged twenty-seven to forty-four, who showed no previous heart problems. The increased heart rate and blood pressure appear to increase the demand for oxygen.

POINT VALUE	QUESTION	ANSWER
30	Which drug interferes with immediate memory and intellectual performance?	Marijuana

Many studies have shown that marijuana interferes with learning and other cognitive functions. Recent memory, short-term memory, and the ability to concentrate are all impaired. The higher the dose, the greater the effect.

POINT VALUE	QUESTION	ANSWER
40	Any chemical substance that brings about physical, emotional, and mental changes in people is a _____.	Drug

Many people take drugs for the pleasure produced. Medicine is taken to ease symptoms of a disease.

POINT VALUE	QUESTION	ANSWER
50	All of the following are drugs: alcohol, tobacco, caffeine, and smokeless tobacco.	True

It is important to note that although alcohol and caffeine are not viewed as chemicals, they are, in fact, drugs to which people become addicted.

POINT VALUE	QUESTION	ANSWER
60	What is the most commonly abused drug today?	Alcohol

Alcohol has the most serious health implications for our society. So much emphasis is placed on the other drugs that many fail to realize that heavy drinking and alcoholism are our most serious adolescent and adult drug problems. With teens, this is often compounded by the use of marijuana, which leads to greater impairment.

POINT VALUE	QUESTION	ANSWER
70	One third of the population is addicted to _____.	Cigarettes

Smoking is the single most preventable cause of disease in the United States today. Smoking increases the risk of emphysema, bronchitis, and lung cancer.

POINT VALUE	QUESTION	ANSWER
80	Barbiturates are called uppers and amphetamines are called downers.	False

Barbiturates are called downers and amphetamines uppers. The effects of depressants are similar to the effects of alcohol. Small amounts produce calmness; larger amounts cause slurred speech, staggering gait, and altered perception. Large doses can cause respiratory depression, coma, and death. When regular users quit abruptly, they may develop withdrawal symptoms, ranging from restlessness, insomnia, and anxiety to convulsions and death.

POINT VALUE	QUESTION	ANSWER
90	Which drug can cause dis-orientation for up to twelve hours?	LSD

LSD causes illusions and hallucinations. Physical effects include dilated pupils, elevated body temperature, loss of control and appetite, and tremors.

POINT VALUE	QUESTION	ANSWER
100	The best remedy for a hangover is A. gradual amounts of coffee. B. a cold bath or shower. C. aspirin and water. D. rest.	D

Alcohol is responsible for the hangover. The hangover will persist until the alcohol has been absorbed through the digestive tract and broken down through metabolism. More alcohol and other drugs will aggravate and lengthen the problem.

CHEMICALS AND YOU

POINT VALUE	QUESTION	ANSWER
10	Marijuana cigarettes can produce as much tar in your lungs as two cigarettes.	True

Marijuana is deeply inhaled and the smoke retained in the lungs for several seconds. Thus, each time a joint equal in weight to a popular high-tar cigarette is smoked this way, the user inhales four times as much tar as that from a tobacco cigarette.

POINT VALUE	QUESTION	ANSWER
20	A withdrawal symptom from coffee most people experience is _____.	Headaches

People become addicted to caffeine just as they can to other chemicals.

POINT VALUE	QUESTION	ANSWER
30	Which of the following substances stays longest in human cells and tissues? A. Nicotine B. Marijuana (THC) C. Heroin D. Cocaine	B

Measurable amounts of chemicals from a single joint of marijuana are detectable in fat cells for a month.

POINT VALUE	QUESTION	ANSWER
40	Long-term use of which of the following can produce memory and speech difficulties (e.g., stuttering, an inability to articulate or speak at all): A. Cocaine B. Phencyclidine (PCP) C. Marijuana D. Barbiturates	B

Phencyclidine (PCP) interrupts the functions of the neocortex, the area of the brain that controls the intellect and keeps the instincts in check. Mood disorders and violent behavior typically occur. Because the drug blocks pain receptors, violent PCP episodes could result in injuries to oneself. Chronic PCP use results in speech and memory problems that can last from six months to a year.

POINT VALUE	QUESTION	ANSWER
50	Those most at risk for chemical addiction are A. pregnant women. B. children of alcoholics. C. wine drinkers. D. alcohol drinkers. E. None of the above.	B

As more genetic research is conducted, the findings are beginning to show that heredity plays a part in addiction. Thus, children of alcoholics are more at risk because of the increased likelihood that this condition is inherited.

POINT VALUE	QUESTION	ANSWER
60	One marijuana joint can decrease some lung functions as much as smoking _____ cigarettes. A. 30 B. 16 C. 100 D. 4	B

Marijuana contains more cancer-causing agents than cigarettes.

DRUGS OK?

POINT VALUE	QUESTION	ANSWER
10	More youth abuse drugs in the United States than in any other country.	True

Drug use in the United States is found among students in the city and country, among the rich and poor, and among the middle class. Drug problems exist in elementary, middle, and high schools. The drug problem in this country is ten times that of Japan. Sixty-one percent of high school seniors have used drugs. Thirteen percent of seniors used cocaine last year.

POINT VALUE	QUESTION	ANSWER
20	The best way to help someone who is chemically addicted is to do things that will make him/her feel good and reduce the stresses in his/her life.	False

When a person continuously makes excuses for and takes responsibility from the chemically dependent person, he/she enables the chemical dependency to continue. Although the enabler's intentions may be good, it keeps the chemically dependent person from facing any consequences because of chemical use.

POINT VALUE	QUESTION	ANSWER
30	Cocaine is only psychologically addictive.	False

For many years, people thought that cocaine was only psychologically addictive. However, given the drug's effects on the brain's reward system, it appears to be physically addictive as well. It stimulates the brain's reward system directly. In animals, cocaine is more reinforcing than any other abused drug, so much so that the animal continues to choose it over all other drugs until death from overdose occurs.

POINT VALUE	QUESTION	ANSWER
40	Women who are heavy smokers A. bear low-birth babies B. can control their smoking better than men C. have nicer complexions. D. All of the above	A

Birth weight, body length, and head circumference of infants whose mother smoked during pregnancy are less than those for infants whose mothers did not smoke. Other complications, both before and after pregnancy, are more frequent in mothers who smoke.

POINT VALUE	QUESTION	ANSWER
50	Marijuana enhances memory.	False

A number of studies have shown that marijuana impedes long- and short-term memory. Many young children who use marijuana show a lack of motivation in school and in extracurricular activities. They withdraw socially and begin limiting their associations to other drug users.

POINT VALUE	QUESTION	ANSWER
60	AIDS can be spread by A. sexual contact B. sharing needles C. kissing D. A & B only E. All of the above	D

Current findings seem to indicate that the AIDS virus must enter the bloodstream directly to be transmitted. Thus, the primary modes of transmittal appear to be sexual contact, blood transfusions, and the sharing of needles by intravenous drug users.

POINT VALUE	QUESTION	ANSWER
70	Four of the five leading causes of death are related to A. alcoholism B. cocaine use C. cigarette smoking D. PCP use	A

Heart disease, one of the four leading causes of death, is related to alcoholism in some people. Some cancers also appear to be related to alcoholism. Average life span of an alcoholic is fifty-nine years of age.

POINT VALUE	QUESTION	ANSWER
80	Which of the following is found in nicotine? A. Carbon monoxide B. Carcinogens C. Traces of arsenic D. B & C only E. All of the above	E

Smoking is related to a number of diseases and accidents. These include household fires and pulmonary disease, such as bronchitis and pneumonia.

POINT VALUE	QUESTION	ANSWER
90	Give one street name for amphetamines.	Speed Black Beauties Uppers Ups Pep Pills Co-pilots Bumblebees Hearts Benzedrine Dexedrine Footballs Biphetamine

Amphetamine injections can create a sudden increase in blood pressure, resulting in strokes, high fever, or heart failure.

POINT VALUE	QUESTION	ANSWER
100	People who do not use intoxicating chemicals before their twentieth birthday A. are more likely to become chemically addicted. B. are less likely to become chemically addicted than those who use intoxicating chemicals earlier. C. will not become addicted. D. None of the above.	B

Because of weight and metabolism, teens are more likely to become intoxicated by consuming lower amounts of alcohol than older drinkers. Also, teens who are children of alcoholics are at high risk for addiction. Adolescent addiction sometimes occurs within one month compared to adult addiction which might take longer.

DRUG BOUTIQUE

POINT VALUE	QUESTION	ANSWER
10	Terminally ill cancer patients are often given morphine, a prescribed pain medication, to lessen their pain.	True

Terminally ill patients are often given powerful pain killers to ease the pain often associated with cancer. These should only be prescribed by a physician, and patients should be monitored closely. Morphine is an opiate derived directly from the opium poppy. Heroin is also derived from the opium poppy and is usually injected, gives a temporary high, and is quite addictive.

POINT VALUE	QUESTION	ANSWER
20	Teens use drugs most of the time at school.	False

Teens have become very aware of the policies for drug use at school. Consequently, not as many teens are actually using or abusing chemicals at schools. This, however, does not mean that they are not using. Instead, many teens are using elsewhere.

POINT VALUE	QUESTION	ANSWER
30	The main ingredient in alcohol is A. ethyl alcohol. B. acetic acid. C. carbon alcohol. D. THC.	A

Ethyl alcohol is the active ingredient in wine, beer, and liquor. In small doses, it has a calming effect. Alcohol affects the liver, brain, and heart.

POINT VALUE	QUESTION	ANSWER
40	Narcotics are used as A. sedatives. B. pain killers. C. enhancers of creativity. D. weight reducers.	B

Narcotics act in a similar way as barbiturates. They are derived from opium and are highly addictive. They are primarily used as pain killers. They depress the central nervous system and can make people both physically and psychologically addicted.

POINT VALUE	QUESTION	ANSWER
50	Which of the following is unrelated to alcohol metabolism? A. Age B. Brand of alcohol C. Sex (male or female) D. Weight E. Number of drinks	B

Age, weight, sex, and number of drinks are all related to alcohol metabolism. Teens are more likely to become intoxicated than an adult who drinks the same amount. Body weight and size have a lot to do with this.

POINT VALUE	QUESTION	ANSWER
60	Since the U. S. Surgeon General's Office declared that cigarette smoking is hazardous to health, smoking has A. declined significantly. B. declined slightly. C. increased. D. declined among women.	C

Evidence shows that young men are smoking less, but women of all ages are smoking more.

POINT VALUE	QUESTION	ANSWER

70

Most adolescent cocaine users
are
A. white males
B. sixteen years of age
C. black males
D. All of the above
E. A & B only

E

Data from the cocaine national hotline indicate that 83 percent of cocaine users are male. Their average age is 16.2 years. Many are from upper-income families. Three quarters missed days from school due to drug use. Many encountered problems, such as expulsion from school.

POINT VALUE	QUESTION	ANSWER

80

Cocaine and alcohol are
similar in that both produce
an initial high followed by
a low.

True

The high experienced with cocaine lasts for only a few minutes. The crash leaves the individual depressed and irritable.

POINT VALUE	QUESTION	ANSWER

90

Cocaine is similar to diet
pills and other stimulant
drugs in that it increases
the appetite.

False

Cocaine is a white powder that is made from the cocoa bush, which is grown in South America. Smoking cocaine increases the chances that users will experience anxiety, extreme agitation, weight loss, sleeplessness, and hallucinations (feeling, hearing, and seeing things that are not there).

90 Appendix III

POINT VALUE	QUESTION	ANSWER
100	The most abused drug in the United States today is _____.	Alcohol

So much attention is given to the abuse of other drugs in this country that most people still fail to realize that the most abused drug in the United States is alcohol. Both adults and youth abuse this drug more than any other drug.

OUNCE OF PREVENTION

POINT VALUE	QUESTION	ANSWER
10	Health costs for alcoholics are three times greater than that of the general population.	True

Because of all the ills which accompany alcoholism, such as cirrhosis of the liver, health costs for alcoholics are at least three times that of the general population. The problems cause lost man hours to employers, and a large percentage of health costs are going to other illnesses related to alcohol addiction. Employee assistance programs are aimed at these problems.

POINT VALUE	QUESTION	ANSWER
20	Alcoholism and drug deaths are the sixth leading cause of death in the United States.	False

It is, in fact, the third leading cause, only preceded by heart attacks and cancer.

POINT VALUE	QUESTION	ANSWER
30	Nearly 10,000 persons died last year in the United States as a result of alcohol-related accidents.	False

The reality is that 24,000 - 25,000 people died in the United States as a result of alcohol-related deaths.

POINT VALUE	QUESTION	ANSWER
40	Al-Anon is the national headquarters for Alcoholics Anonymous.	False

Al-Anon is a support group for people impacted by the alcoholism of others. In these groups, men and women come to a greater understanding of alcoholism and learn that their role is not to control the alcoholic.

POINT VALUE	QUESTION	ANSWER
50	An "enabler" is someone who helps the chemically addicted get well.	False

An "enabler" is someone who makes excuses and solves problems for an addicted person. This behavior often prevents many chemically addicted persons from seeking help.

POINT VALUE	QUESTION	ANSWER
60	The "Twelve Steps" of AA and Al-Anon teach people to control everything in their lives.	False

To the contrary, Alcoholics Anonymous (AA) and Al-Anon help teach people that, in fact, they can't control everything in their lives, including alcohol or the alcoholic. Instead, people come to understand that a power (whatever they choose to call it) higher than they gives them the spiritual strength to let go of alcohol (for the alcoholic) and "trying to control the alcoholic" (for the Al-Anon affected by the drinking).

POINT VALUE	QUESTION	ANSWER
70	Intervention is concerned about getting help for persons affected by chemical addiction.	True

Intervention is a process whereby others--family, friends, lovers, police, courts, etc.--use external leverage to get the chemically addicted into treatment. Often, ultimatums or bottom lines are given which push the addicted person into treatment; e.g., "Get help or get out!" However, bottom lines which are not intended to be followed through should not be given.

POINT VALUE	QUESTION	ANSWER
80	Prevention is best accomplished by scaring people about the dangers of drugs.	False

During the 1960s, people all over found out that scare tactics had virtually no impact on eliminating problems with chemical abuse or addiction. This approach is much too simplistic in dealing with a problem as complex as chemical addiction.

POINT VALUE	QUESTION	ANSWER
90	If we teach youth good life skills and positive self-images, they will be less likely to become alcoholics when they drink as adults.	False

An individual can be taught all the life skills necessary for functioning well in society; however, if that individual is genetically at risk because alcoholism runs in his/her family, if he/she drinks, he /she is more likely to become addicted regardless of life skills taught.

POINT VALUE	QUESTION	ANSWER
100	Most school-aged students are first exposed to drugs by the fourth grade.	True

A recent *Weekly Reader* survey found that by the fourth grade most students have been exposed to drugs.

NEVER-NEVER LAND

POINT VALUE	QUESTION	ANSWER
10	Only 45 percent of alcoholics are on skid row.	False

Most people operate under the myth that most alcoholics are on skid row. However, the reality is that only 3 to 5 percent of alcoholics are on skid row.

POINT VALUE	QUESTION	ANSWER
20	A "blackout" is when someone passes out from drinking alcohol.	False

A blackout is a loss of recall or any memory of events which have occurred. Driving home from a party and not remembering the drive or talking to friends at a party and not remembering the conversation is a blackout. In other words, a blackout is an inability to recall facts, events, and information because of drinking.

POINT VALUE	QUESTION	ANSWER
30	Once an alcoholic, always an alcoholic.	True

Alcoholism is a disease and, just as diabetes or hypertension, can be controlled but not cured. Thus, we hear the saying, "Once an alcoholic, always an alcoholic." It is not meant in a "put down" fashion, but rather should serve as a reminder that it is a treatable disease that does not have to lead to death.

POINT VALUE	QUESTION	ANSWER
40	Chemical dependency is primarily a problem among A. teens. B. skid row alcoholics. C. urban poverty areas. D. middle-class professionals. E. all social classes.	E

Chemical abuse and use are equal opportunity activities that cut across race, culture, and socioeconomic groups.

POINT VALUE	QUESTION	ANSWER
50	Alcohol, cigarettes, and other drugs consumed by pregnant women A. are filtered by the placenta before entering the fetus' bloodstream. B. usually kill the fetus directly. C. affect the fetus directly. D. are usually removed by antitoxins in the mother's bloodstream.	C

When a mother consumes drugs during pregnancy, the fetus is directly impacted. Not only is the fetus intoxicated, but it is also unable to metabolize and detoxify those chemicals because its system is underdeveloped.

POINT VALUE	QUESTION	ANSWER
60	It is possible to become addicted to A. coffee. B. marijuana. C. over-the-counter diet pills. D. cigarettes. E. Any of these.	E

All of these are drugs; consequently, people can become addicted to any of them.

POINT VALUE	QUESTION	ANSWER
70	Drugs, such as LSD and certain kinds of mushrooms, are called _____.	Hallucinogens

LSD causes illusions and hallucinations.

POINT VALUE	QUESTION	ANSWER
80	Crack is made from cocaine and can be cut with baking soda and is, therefore, less dangerous than cocaine.	False

Crack, or freebase rock, is just as addictive as cocaine. The physical effects include dilated pupils, increased pulse rate, elevated blood pressure, insomnia, seizures, and loss of appetite.

POINT VALUE	QUESTION	ANSWER
90	Preteens often use inhalants, such as glue, gasoline, etc., because they are inexpensive and cause less damage to body organs.	False

These substances cause a great deal of tissue damage. Some of the industrial solvents are highly toxic to liver function. Other inhaled materials can coat lung tissue, blocking oxygen transfer; thus, while these substances may be cheap, they do a great deal of bodily harm.

96   Appendix III

POINT VALUE	QUESTION	ANSWER
100	Although _____ has not been a popularly abused drug in the general population, it has been widely used in some areas. In the Washington, D.C. area, it became the principal reason for teens being admitted to psychiatric hospitals. The behaviors produced are usually bizarre acts involving violent behavior. What is the drug?	PCP

PCP is also called "angel dust." It has never been an extremely popular drug. Its effects include numbness of extremities and intoxication. Perception is distorted, and paranoid thinking often occurs.

DESIGNER GENES

POINT VALUE	QUESTION	ANSWER
10	According to a 1987 Gallup Poll, one out of six families has someone who is addicted to chemicals.	False

One out of four. This is a primary reason why the need for treatment of families impacted by addiction is so vitally important.

POINT VALUE	QUESTION	ANSWER
20	Alcoholism was declared a disease by the American Medical Association.	True

For many years, people felt that alcoholism was a problem of will. Today, the research findings support the fact that alcoholism is a disease.

POINT VALUE	QUESTION	ANSWER
30	Alcoholism is a primary, chronic, and fatal condition.	True

Alcoholism is a chronic, progressive, and incurable disease characterized by loss of control over alcohol and other sedatives. *Chronic* means that it lasts a long time, and *progressive* means that it goes on and on; that is, as the alcoholic continues to drink, the disease gets worse. Social drinking is never an option for an alcoholic.

POINT VALUE	QUESTION	ANSWER
40	Certain ethnic groups are more susceptible to alcoholism than others.	True

Native Americans, Irish, blacks, and Hispanics are at greater risk, based on the data, than such groups as Italians and Jews.

POINT VALUE	QUESTION	ANSWER
50	Children of alcoholics are less likely to become alcoholics because they have seen what it does to people.	False

Knowing what happened in their own family is not enough. If they have a predisposition to alcoholism (and many will if it runs in their family), then they are at risk.

POINT VALUE	QUESTION	ANSWER
60	Children of alcoholics often need treatment as much as the alcoholic.	True

Since alcoholism is a family disease, all members need treatment. In an addicted home, all family members begin to respond and interact in unhealthy ways to survive in the addicted home. Only through treatment can these issues be addressed.

POINT VALUE	QUESTION	ANSWER
70	There are approximately 25-30 million children of alcoholics in our country.	True

Many estimate the figure to be higher. However, this figure alone makes a statement about the need for family treatment. Without such intervention, these children of alcoholics will bring the same unhealthy behaviors to their families, and the pattern will continue.

POINT VALUE	QUESTION	ANSWER
90	Many famous comedians, such as Jackie Gleason, Suzanne Sommers, and Carole Burnett, are children of alcoholics.	True

Many famous comedians were "mascots" in their addicted families. They tried to relieve the stress and tension in their families with humor.

POINT VALUE	QUESTION	ANSWER
100	What is the average life span for a Native American male in Oklahoma? A. Sixty years old B. Fifty-five years old C. Forty-eight years old D. None of the above	C

An article in the *Daily Oklahoman* pointed out this startling statistic. The reason seems either directly or indirectly (homicides, suicides) tied to alcoholism. Because the introduction of alcohol to the Native American culture is so recent, as a group they seem less able to metabolize alcohol.

Appendix IV

Session XVII: Drugs and Society
Session XVIII: Drugs and Family

Compelling Future in 3-D: Discovery Decisions Determination, A Leadership Training and Drug and Alcohol Prevention and Intervention Curriculum

Overview of Session XVII

UNIT: Chemical Awareness

LESSON: Impact of Chemicals on Society

GOAL(S):

To help participants become sensitive to the scope of problems related to chemical abuse and addiction

CONTENT OF SESSION

ACTIVITY:

1. Game Show Review and Wrap-up

TIME:

60 minutes

100

Compelling Future in 3-D:
A Leadership Training and Drug and Alcohol Prevention and Intervention Curriculum, 1988

Overview of Session XVIII

ACTIVITY: Game Show Wrap-up and Review   TIME: 60 Minutes

MATERIALS: Film: Soft Is the Heart of a Child   VOCABULARY:

OBJECTIVES:

1. To help participants differentiate facts from fiction regarding the impact of chemicals on the individual, the family, and society
2. To help participants assess the impact of chemical addiction as a barrier to realizing one's compelling future

PROCEDURE

The facilitator should open group discussion by selecting item-by-item questions from the Game Board Show. Participants should be asked to repeat their responses. Facilitators should then provide additional information and facts and engage participants in further discussion.

After discussing all questions, participants should be asked individually how becoming addicted to chemicals could be a barrier for them in reaching their compelling future. If it has already become a problem for anyone in the group, they should privately place it on their road map; and if they want to discuss it with the facilitator at some future date, they should be encouraged to do so.

If time permits, the film *Soft Is the Heart of a Child* can be shown. This film portrays the impact of chemical addiction on the family.

ACTIVITY: The Family Trap   TIME: 60 Minutes

MATERIALS: Rope or Cord   VOCABULARY:
           Sharon Wegscheider's   Co-dependency
           Handout on the Family Trap   Lost Child
                                            Family Hero
                                            Chief Enabler
                                            Mascot
                                            Scapegoat
                                            Dysfunctional

OBJECTIVES:

1. To help participants assess the impact of chemical dependency on all
   members of a family system
2. To help participants identify the roles which emerge in a chemically
   dependent family system
3. To help participants identify behavioral characteristics which
   accompany these roles

PROCEDURE

Begin this session by passing out the handout by Sharon Wegscheider on
the family trap (Lost Child, Chief Enabler, Mascot, and Scapegoat).
Explain to participants that this is a model for dysfunctional families
(unhealthy families where boundaries, roles, and rules are blurred, as
discussed in Session IV). However, sometimes each of us might play
these roles even if our family is healthy.

The facilitator should spend fifteen minutes reviewing these roles and
entertain questions from the participants. The facilitator should then say,

I WOULD LIKE FOR YOU TO PAUSE FOR A MOMENT AND
REFLECT ON HOW PLAYING EACH OF THESE ROLES IN A
FAMILY MIGHT HELP OR BE A BARRIER IN REALIZING ONE'S
COMPELLING FUTURE.

The following responses might emerge as barriers:

1. *Chief Enabler*--This person is often so busy taking care of the needs of the chemically addicted person that there is little time to take care of their own wishes, wants, and needs. When individuals are willing to totally ignore their own wishes, needs, and wants to appease and control the chemically addicted person, they are called co-dependents.

2. *Family Hero*--This person is often so busy trying to bring self-worth to the family system by achieving success he/she often fails to get in touch with what he/she wants. Thus, while a compelling future is realized, it is often someone else's vision rather than the person's own.

3. *Scapegoat*--This person often takes the focus off the chemically addicted person by acting out or becoming chemically addicted. This person is likely to never realize his/her compelling future without intervention because he/she is constantly creating barriers for himself/herself.

4. *Lost Child*--This person often withdraws so much from society that little energy is directed at realizing a compelling future.

5. *Mascot*--This person uses humor to relieve the stress from the family system. He/she is similar to Peter Pan in that he/she never grows up. This lack of maturity can often serve as a barrier to the realization of a compelling future.

The facilitator should now say the following:

LET'S ROLE PLAY WHAT ACTUALLY HAPPENS TO A FAMILY SYSTEM WHEN THERE IS A CHEMICALLY DEPENDENT PERSON IN THE FAMILY. THIS ROLE PLAY IS OFTEN CALLED THE FAMILY TRAP. AFTER THE ROLE PLAY, WE WILL DISCUSS WHAT WE HAVE OBSERVED AND WHY YOU THINK THIS ROLE PLAY IS CALLED THE FAMILY TRAP. I NEED THE FOLLOWING VOLUNTEERS:

A CHEMICALLY DEPENDENT PERSON
CHIEF ENABLER
FAMILY HERO

SCAPEGOAT
LOST CHILD
MASCOT

Arrange the participants in the following manner for the role play that should take no longer than ten minutes:

1. Have the chemically dependent person stand on something sturdy, such as a table. Other family members remain standing on the floor.

2. Tie the rope or cord around the chemically dependent person's waist and connect each of the other family members in the same manner, leaving a length of 4 to 5 feet between them.

3. Provide extra length for the lost child who should be as far away from the family as possible.

4. Ask the chief enabler to begin to role play by pleading with the chemically addicted person to stop drug use.

5. Ask all other family members to role play their response based on the roles defined in the previous discussion.

6. The facilitator should ask the chemically dependent person to step down and move as far in another direction as possible. All family members should then move with him/her without breaking the rope. This serves to illustrate how all family members play a role in maintaining the dysfunctional family system.

As the role play is being presented, the facilitator should periodically point out how all family members are tied to each other and support directly or indirectly the chemically addicted person. There is an invisible, unhealthy bond connecting the family members to each other. He/she should also point out the problems created in communication with dysfunctional families.

At the end of the role play, the facilitator should say the following:

I AM NOW GOING TO PUT THIS ENTIRE FAMILY INTO TREATMENT.

The chief enabler decides to get help. The facilitator should untie the chief enabler from the chemically dependent person. This process should continue until each family member has gone into treatment. The chemically dependent person is then forced to seek help because the family is no longer willing to support his/her unhealthy behaviors. The facilitator should point out to the group that recovery for a dysfunctional family is a painful and long process because all family members must learn to relate to each other and themselves differently and in more healthy ways.

The facilitator should be sensitive to the fact that a role play such as this might open up personal issues for many participants. He/she should be prepared to provide time after class for further discussion and to refer participants for additional assistance and support, if needed, to outside agencies.

Now engage the class in discussion on what they observed from the family trap and why they feel the role play is called, "A Family Trap." General responses should include the following understanding:

> Family members feel helpless to break ties and are thus trapped in an
> unhealthy situation.

The facilitator can also point out that communication is often indirect, and children in this situation often tell white lies. They have learned that to cope with the chemically dependent person often means skirting around the issues. In fact, their very survival often depends on this.

Additional questions can be entertained at this time.

Glossary

Chevrat noar: A term which refers to a peer group community of Israeli youth, ages thirteen to sixteen, which was absorbed in *kibbutzim* during the period after World War II. The members usually were from the same ethnic group(s) coming from Europe and North Africa en masse. The task of the *chevrat noar* was to help people tackle their emotional and social problems as individuals and develop coherent and self-disciplined groups.

Garin: A core or nucleus group of young people who represent an original seed group which settles in a kibbutz or other collective settlement. Many Israelis join a *garin* before army service and settle in a kibbutz with it immediately after they finish their service.

Kibbutzim: The Israeli collective settlements. The *kibbutzim* were used to settle survivors of the Holocaust and absorb large numbers of North African and Middle Eastern Jewish youth after World War II, supplying a supportive and idealistic environment for problem youth.

Madricha (plural *madrichim*): A peer group model who directly supervises the *chevrat noar* on a day-to-day basis and guides the group through the various stages of its development by exerting authority as a charismatic leader. He/she lives at the same settlement where the group lives, usually as a member. A part-time *madricha* assists a group in its organizational work and activities once or twice a week. He/she is often paid by a youth movement or has volunteered his/her services during a pre- or postarmy national service period. He/she may live in the city or be a kibbutz inhabitant who has moved to a town temporarily.

Nachal: The pioneering Israeli Army units' organization which set up or added to the personnel of *kibbutzim* under the auspices of the Israeli Army, the Israeli youth movement, and the Jewish Agency.

Sephardic: A Jew whose origins were in North Africa, the Middle East, Greece, Turkey, Italy, and the Iberian Peninsula. This group is also referred to as Eastern.

Youth Aliyah: The agency whose original task was to save Jewish youth from fascism in the 1930s but later extended its activities to rescuing and absorbing families in danger elsewhere in the world. In the context of this study, its activity of working with poor troubled Jewish youth in Israel is stressed.

Bibliography

Austin, James B. and John Reaves. *How to Find Help for a Troubled Kid*. New York: Holt and Co., 1990.

Barnes, Tom. "Mayor Pitches Anti-Crime Program." *The Pittsburgh-Post Gazette* (April 16, 1994), pp. C1, C7.

Berne, Patricia and Louis Savary. *Building Self-Esteem in Children*. New York: The Continuum Publishing Co., 1987.

Biscoe, Belinda, John Mayfield, and Carol Wakely. *A Chance for Youth: A Leadership Curriculum*. Oklahoma City: The United States Department of Health and Human Services, 1992.

Brown, Claude. "The Language of Violence." *The Pittsburgh-Post Gazette* (May 28, 1994), p. B3.

Fanfani, Mario D., editor. *Alternative Education*. Garden City, NY: Doubleday Co., Inc. 1976.

Frank, Ivan C. *Children in Chaos*. Westport, CT: Praeger Publishing Co., 1992.

Fuoco, Linda. "Problems at Shuman Steeped in Violence." *The Pittsburgh Post-Gazette* (March 29, 1993), pp. A1, A2.

Hemmings, Ray, editor. *Children's Freedom: A. S. Neill and the Evolution of the Summerhill Idea*. New York: Schocken Books, 1973.

Jones, R. Lamont, Jr. "Blount's Plan Gets Mixed Reactions." *The Pittsburgh Post-Gazette* (May 4, 1994a), p. B1.

Jones, R. Lamont, Jr. "Northside Gangs Call Truce." *The Pittsburgh Post-Gazette* (March 26, 1994b), p. A12.

Kozol, Jonathan. *Death at an Early Age*. New York: Penguin Books, 1990.

Kozol, Jonathan. *Savage Inequalities*. New York: Crown Publishing Co., 1990.

Lee, Carmen. "Violence Targeted by P.S.E.A." *The Pittsburgh Post-Gazette* (May 22, 1994), p. B7.

Mann, Cynthia. "Donna Shalala Spends Thanksgiving in Israel."   *The Jewish Chronicle of Pittsburgh* (December 1, 1994), p. 37.

Marriott, Michelle. "For Minority Youth, 40 Ounces of Trouble."   *The New York Times* (April 16, 1993), p. A1.

NBC Evening News, 1994.

Near, Henry. *The History of the Kibbutz Movement.* Oxford, England: The Oxford Publishing Co., 1994.

Neill, A. S. *Summerhill.* New York: Hart Publishing Co., 1960.

Reaves, Tim. "State Crime Rate Falls Again." *The Pittsburgh Post-Gazette* (November 17, 1994), pp. A1, A7.

Ritter, Joseph.   "Youth Rehabilitation Program."   A report to the International Conference of Jewish Communal Service, Child Care Workshop, Tel Aviv, 1973.

Robenstein, C. and Fred Shultz, editors. "Education Reform and At-Risk Students," in *Multicultural Education.* Guilford, CT: Dushkin Publishing Co., 1994.

Rossi, Nora, and Tom Cole, translators. *Letters to a Teacher.* New York: Vantage Books, 1971.

Scholastic Scope, the Teacher's Edition (March 12, 1993), p. 1.

Treaster, Joseph. "Beyond Probation: Breaking the Cycle of Juvenile Arrest." *The New York Times* (December 29, 1994), pp. A1, A10.

Tunley, Roul. *Kids, Crimes and Chaos: A World Report on Juvenile Delinquency.* New York: Dell Publishing Co., 1962.

Wilkerson, Isabel. "Doing Whatever It Takes to Save a Child." *The New York Times* (December 30, 1994), pp. A1, A10.

Williams, A. "Integration Turns 40." *Maturity* (April/May, 1994), pp. 24-33.

Wolin, Stephen J. and Sybil Wolin. *The Resilient Self.* New York: Villard Books, 1993.

Zuchinno, David. "Heeding the Call of the Streets." *The Philadelphia Inquirer* (November 13, 1994), pp. A1, A22, A23.

Index

Summerhill, 4, 13, 15, 16, 32,
48, 49

Teachers, xii, xiv, xv, 1, 3, 4,
6, 13, 14, 15, 16, 19, 23,
24, 25, 26, 27, 28, 31, 32,
33, 34, 36, 37, 38, 40, 43,
44, 45, 49, 50, 54, 59, 60
Texas, xv, 1, 17, 18, 19, 48
Three Rivers Youth, 1, 3, 23,
59

Urban, xii, 1, 2, 7, 9, 14, 17,
25, 26, 40, 44, 59, 60

Violence, xiii, xiv, 3, 4, 6, 19,
20, 31, 34, 35, 41, 43, 44,
45, 59, 60
Volunteers, xi, xiv, 1, 5, 6, 9,
16, 17, 18, 26, 33, 39, 50

Wagon Train Program, 55
Warehousing, xiii, 10, 18, 37,
39, 60
Wolin, Stephen, 51
Wolin, Sybil, 51

Youth Aliyah, 1, 4, 5, 9, 10,
16, 17, 18, 32, 40, 45, 47,
48, 50

About the Author

IVAN C. FRANK is a noted American educator and expert on high-risk youth. Frank has been teaching in high schools, colleges, and youth centers for over 30 years and currently runs workshops on teaching high-risk youth. His previous books include *Children in Chaos* (Praeger, 1992), and *The Cycle of Learning* (1984).

ISBN 0-275-95267-3

90000>

EAN

9 780275 952679

HARDCOVER BAR CODE